Tracy and Hepburn Speak:

KATHARINE HEPBURN:

"I always had this terrible antipathy toward the press. I didn't think they had any business to know certain things. And I didn't think the corners of my private life belonged to them. . . . I don't particularly believe in marriage. I'm not even sure that men and women suit each other enough to live in the same house."

SPENCER TRACY:

"I don't think I've got an unusual fear of death, but I can't watch any film with Clark Gable or Bogie or any actor I knew well. Maybe I'm just too conscious of time passing, especially since I got so ill. . . . I agree with Laurence Olivier that it's a crashing bore to talk about acting. Who the hell knows anything about it? I don't."

ABOUT THE AUTHOR

Roy Newquist's interest in writers and performers has led to the publication of three collections of interviews, COUNTERPOINT, SHOWCASE, *and* CONVERSATIONS. *In addition he has written a great number of articles for Magazines such as* McCall's *and* Cosmopolitan. *Wisconsin-born and educated, Newquist is at present literary editor of* Chicago's American *and a widely syndicated columnist. He lives in Park Forest, Illinois, with his wife, three children, and a 140-pound Rhodesian Ridgeback name Simba.*

A SPECIAL KIND OF MAGIC

Roy Newquist

A SPECIAL KIND OF MAGIC

A Pyramid Book

Published by arrangement with Rand McNally & Company

Pyramid edition published August 1972

ISBN 0-515-02767-7

Library of Congress Catalog Card Number: 68-13405

Printed in the United States of America

Pyramid Books are published by Pyramid Communications, Inc.
Its trademarks, consisting of the word "Pyramid" and the portrayal of a pyramid, are registered in the United States Patent Office.

Pyramid Communications, Inc., 919 Third Avenue,
New York, N.Y. 10022

Contents

ROY NEWQUIST • 9

STANLEY KRAMER • 16

KATHARINE HEPBURN • 55

SIDNEY POITIER • 115

KATHARINE HOUGHTON • 130

SPENCER TRACY • 146

Illustrations

The five principals involved in A SPECIAL KIND OF MAGIC

Katharine Hepburn in *Morning Glory;* Spencer Tracy in *Captains Courageous;* Katharine Hepburn as Jo in *Little Women* and with Ginger Rogers in *Stage Door*

Spencer Tracy as Father Flanagan in *Boys' Town;* Cary Grant and Katharine Hepburn in *Holiday;* Spencer Tracy and Katharine Hepburn in *Keeper of the Flame*

Tracy and Hepburn in *Sea of Grass;* in *Adam's Rib;* and in *State of the Union;* Together again in *Pat and Mike;* Humphrey Bogart with Hepburn in *African Queen*

Tracy and Hepburn in their last picture together, *Guess Who's Coming to Dinner*

On the set of *Guess Who's Coming to Dinner*

Stanley Kramer and Sidney Poitier, Cecil Kellaway, Spencer Tracy and Katharine Hepburn; Aunt and

Niece relaxing between takes; Katharine Houghton and Sidney Poitier in scene from movie

Poitier and Tracy having a talk; Katharine Hepburn in her favorite hat; Katharine Houghton, Hepburn and Tracy preparing for a take; Scenes from film with Katharine Houghton and Sidney Poitier; the two Katharines in tender scene

Scene in drive-in with Spencer Tracy and Katharine Hepburn; Sidney Poitier and Katharine Houghton in one of the final scenes

Roy Newquist

THIS BOOK is not a history of Hollywood nor a commentary on the film industry. No final verdicts or pronouncements are made, although I do regard Stanley Kramer's production of *Guess Who's Coming to Dinner* as a pivotal film in Hollywood history. In fact, this book is an accident. I was present on the set throughout the filming of this movie with the intention of doing a series of tape-recordings with the principals, interviews that were later to appear in various magazines.

Gradually, however, I began to realize that a particular set of circumstances and a curious procession of events made me feel as though I had been witnessing, through a juxtaposition of very special kinds of magic, a dramatic microcosm of what Hollywood has been, is, and will be.

Relatively small portions of this book deal with the mechanics of motion picture production. Such material is confined to the comments of intelligent people as they worked together to produce an intelligent film. The bulk of the book, aside from a skimming narrative, consists of what these people say about their lives and careers and the entire world they survey and inhabit. Fortunately, when they talk they are always interesting and often fascinating, for they relate to the principles by which we live as well as virtually all that is important to the motion picture industry.

Who can better explain Stanley Kramer's rough and colorful career as a rebel with a cause than Stanley Kramer himself?

Who is better qualified than Katharine Hepburn to explain her deep-rooted aversion to publicity and the codes that have governed her strong-willed life?

Sidney Poitier discussing Sidney Poitier is a compelling man, whether recalling a "lost" West Indies boyhood or warning us of greater racial turmoil to come unless sweeping changes are made in the hearts of men.

And the freshness and youth of Katharine Houghton and her down-to-earth practicality come through, bright and clear.

Finally, in Spencer Tracy with his tense manner of speech, both humor and sadness are to be found and an oddly gentle personality. Always regarded as a terrible subject for the interviewer (he disliked to talk about himself and refused to theorize about acting), this is probably the most complete interview he ever granted. It was also his last.

What turned a routine assignment into a complex venture? A great number of things, actually, some involved with the film itself, others with production details regarding the film. The most important element, however—the catalyst—was Katharine Hepburn because it was she who inspired the others to talk as freely as they did. Throughout her long career she has loathed publicity and shunned encounter with the press. Over four years ago I approached her for an in-depth taped interview. Politely but firmly she said "no." I persisted, and finally she agreed—only because she would be working again, and because publicity might help her niece, Katharine Houghton.

Miss Hepburn's "unlocking" extended to the press as a whole; naturally this drew more attention to the filming of *Guess Who's Coming to Dinner* than even its strong theme (racial integration through marriage) would have attracted. It proved beyond doubt that Katharine Hepburn's special magic has not diminished over the decades, neither in her personal luster nor in the fascination she holds for all generations.

Led by Miss Hepburn, that other 'holdout" from the press, her great and close friend, Spencer Tracy, sat still for a number of interviews. Sidney Poitier—not noted for accessibility—also complied. Then, as I spoke to Stanley Kramer, I realized that I was getting more than the story of a movie; my tape recorder was collecting rough autobiographies of some of the most important and fascinating personalities in the film industry.

Hollywood, we like to believe, is not noted for films of social significance. Pleasure and profit, not preachment, seem to be its aim. However, critic and public alike frequently forget that excellent "message" films have been produced. Racism, war, alcoholism, anti-Semitism, despotism, poverty, are some of the issues which have been probed, notably *The Birth of a*

Nation, All Quiet on the Western Front, The Grapes of Wrath, Citizen Kane, Gentleman's Agreement, Pinky, The Lost Weekend, and *Home of the Brave.*

Guess Who's Coming to Dinner is *not* the first film to deal with integration; however, it is the first to do so in terms of an honest examination of the problems that arise through intermarriage. It is a comedy, a romance, and a drama. It does not deal with the savage looting and arson that blighted the summer of 1967. With dignity and honesty—but with as much intensity as those hot nights seemed to inspire—it points to the human and humane involvements which transpire above street level.

The film draws its strength from the past, its intensity from the present, its significance from the future. To some degree the American film industry, the acting profession, and our greatest social problem are involved. It is a glimpse of an industry deep in transition as it reflects upon a public in deeper transition and a bold attempt to make the American film speak forthrightly on contemporary issues.

Producer-director Stanley Kramer must be regarded as a catalytic element in Hollywood history if only because he stands as the most influential man to challenge and break big-studio monopoly of talent and properties after World War II made the industry richer than ever and the advent of television made it more terrified than ever. Whether operating on large or small budgets, Kramer has made distinguished, daring films.

Upon a poignant racial theme, he has imposed big-star (Tracy-Hepburn) box-office appeal, the relatively new lure of Sidney Poitier, a star-is-born treatment of Katharine Houghton, and a magnificent screenplay by William Rose. Kramer is backed by big-studio

(Columbia) financing and booking. Yet the film is solidly and intrinsically his own, in contrast with the pictures he produced when he was under contract to that studio during the reign of Harry Cohn.

With more finesse than he displayed with *It's a Mad, Mad, Mad, Mad World,* but with the same daring that motivated *Home of the Brave,* Stanley Kramer has come full circle. He has put a large budget to work in the challenging field of social commentary. This is no small risk; a film with a powerful message is normally given a low budget, thus assuring a reasonable return even if it does not click at the box office. Good box office almost invariably consists of trouble-free entertainment. *Guess Who's Coming to Dinner* should change things, if only a little, by proving that it is possible to insert a message into first-rate entertainment. It is mature, adult entertainment. It is the kind that flourished in the satirical comedy and drama of late eighteenth- and early nineteenth-century France and England.

Spencer Tracy and Katharine Hepburn—simply by their presence—give the film undeniable stature. With the single exception of Elizabeth Taylor, the long era of the superstar passed with the tragic death of Tracy. Tracy and Hepburn made this their last film because they believed in its value as entertainment, and in the message it was to convey, and because of their faith in Stanley Kramer. Scene after scene, fortunately, discloses all the public loved in the eight other films in which they costarred; the puppy-kitten relationship between man and woman regardless of degrees of sophistication; the importance of being moved and mutually attracted as man and woman; the vitality of feeling issues which go beyond private life, consequently forcing participation in the affairs of the community and the world; the humor which alternately alienates us and binds us together. *Guess Who's Coming to Dinner* is the perfect ending for one of the perfect acting companionships any entertainment medium has ever given us. Not only do they appear in the type of roles in which they have long been applauded and loved, they appear in parts which speak strongly for their own fervently expressed liberalism.

Sidney Poitier can be correctly described as riding the crest of the new wave of personalities dominating entertainment in the United States. He is big, black, and beautiful. His talented presence lends dignity and power, not only to the screen, but wherever he is to be observed. He cannot, as a Negro, dismiss riots in Detroit or Newark from his conscience. But he does, as a thoughtful, sensitive, and intelligent man, show us the compassionate and logical society that must come into existence once the ordeals of the riot are over and gone.

Of Katharine Houghton, Stanley Kramer has created a star, and this star may be somewhat in the image of her aunt Katharine Hepburn. I am not a critic, but I find her a delight and hope an auspicious debut is followed by meaty parts in the theater and motion pictures.

The special kinds of magic *Guess Who's Coming to Dinner* contains, deserve reflection. For the sake of art, we hope that it succeeds to a measure that brings similar efforts. For the sake of humanity, we hope that this film, and its successors, help bring about a social sanity we imperatively need. But it is in the heart, after all, where integration will take place, not simply the heart "in love," but the heart unequivocally in love with life. The Greeks had a word for it—*agape*—which reaches out to include the most profound affection and tolerance man can bestow upon his fellows.

Stanley Kramer

SLIM, of medium height, fair skin, soft voice—this is Stanley Kramer. No beret, no cigar, no tendency to sink his bottom deeply into a labeled canvas chair. He's so unlike the prototype of the Hollywood producer-director that only the on-set silence allows his "All right, cut!" to be heard.

He has been, despite those occasions when he got more excited about a project than the public did, and during a period of being at odds with czar Harry Cohn, the most successful independent producer since Goldwyn and Disney.

Only a handful of his films need be mentioned to show his extremely bright place beneath the Hollywood sun: *Champion, Home of the Brave, The Men, Cyrano de Bergerac, High Noon, The Caine Mutiny, The Defiant Ones, On the Beach, Inherit the Wind, Judgment at Nuremberg, It's a Mad, Mad, Mad, Mad World,* and *Ship of Fools.*

His latest film, *Guess Who's Coming to Dinner,* is a more-than-appropriate observance of his twentieth anniversary as an independent producer. A high-powered cast has turned what could have been a "message" film into great entertainment, without losing any of the message. It may well be—both because of its intrinsic strength as a film, and in its daring assault upon racial prejudice—the most important and the best motion picture Stanley Kramer has yet produced or directed.

We discussed his career and how the making of *Guess Who's Coming to Dinner* came about.

STANLEY KRAMER: I'm a complete New York product, as it were. Born there, attended elementary school, De Witt Clinton High School and New York University. The day I was graduated from N.Y.U. I came to California. I had what was called a "junior writer" deal. I was nineteen and Fox had set up a program (more for publicity purposes than for real, I'm afraid) of taking and training young writers from universities. They brought out six of us, and gave us three-month contracts beginning at $80 a week. They said they'd teach us to write for films, but nobody taught us and nobody read what we did. If they had I'm sure they wouldn't have been impressed. At the end of three months, we were all tossed out.

That's how I got into the film business. I found myself three thousand miles away from home in a dastardly year, 1933, without a job. I didn't have any money. My mother had worked as a secretary at Paramount (in New York) for years, had put me through college. Whatever money my family had was lost in the stock-market crash. So I ended up with the chagrin, disillusionment, and disappointment that could only come, in that degree, to a nineteen-year-old who had been given an office and told he must write and being fired three months later.

I knocked around for a while, then got a job back at Fox on the swing gang in the property department. These are the guys who move the furniture on and off the set at night. The job only lasted seven weeks—for a very good reason. On my honor, I didn't know that I was really being a strikebreaker, a scab. The prop men were on strike, and when the strike was settled they fired me. But during that time I'd met a production manager at the studio who called somebody at MGM.

I went into their research department, pasting period pictures of costumes into large volumes—this was for *David Copperfield*. I then got myself transferred into the cutting department and became an assistant film cutter. (First an apprentice, then an assistant.) I worked there for three and a half years, on and off, being laid off and put back on. I wrote some originals which I didn't sell, and that kept me busy, especially when I was laid off.

I finally got transferred to the short subjects department, which contained a lot of people who later became quite distinguished in the industry. Pete Smith was there, doing his own subjects, and this became the root of my next difficulty. Since I'd done some writing, and had film-editing experience, the head of the shorts department thought it would be a good idea if I became Pete Smith's assistant. The trouble was, he didn't talk to Pete Smith about it, so when I arrived on the scene, after my transfer, Smith said, "You know, I really don't want or need you." But the studio felt some obligation, and let me sit around for three or four months doing nothing before letting me go. So after a whirlwind round of assignments, I ended up back on the street having accomplished nothing; I had no screen credits. Since I'd transferred out of the cutting department they wouldn't take me back, so things were tough. I couldn't get a job.

Fortunately, I met Vivian Cosby, a New York playwright sort of down on her luck. She had done some radio writing, so she taught me how, and we teamed up and did guest shots for Rudy Vallee and the Chase and Sanborn Hour, a few Lux Theater adaptations, a few Big Town shows. It was good enough money to manage a living on half the loot. And again I turned out original stories. In those days a lot of writers were doing originals (now there are few) and I sold one or two to what I called the grapefruit circuit—the Republic and Columbia B, C, and D pictures that were made for virtually nothing. For example, I did one titled *Stunt Girl* that used little more than stock footage the studio had on hand, and blended it into a story. I sold that for $400, and they put me on salary for eight weeks at $150 per week, but the film was never made.

One of the radio shows paid off. A producer at MGM, Albert Lewin, thought one of the Lux shows I'd done alone had possibilities. He didn't buy the story, but he brought me to the studio as his assistant. He left MGM after four or five months and formed an independent company with David Loew, releasing through United Artists, and I went with them as their assistant. I made $120 a week as story editor, casting director, production director, and liaison man. They made a picture titled *So Ends Our Night,* adapted from Erich Maria Remarque's novel, *Flotsam,* starring Margaret Sullavan, Fredric March, and Glenn Ford; then Somerset Maugham's *The Moon and Sixpence* with George Sanders. I was the associate producer on both of these.

Then I got all sorts of visions and hallucinations; I

wasn't making any money, I'd always wanted to be a director, and here I was, an associate producer, and by title. I did a lot of casting, I'd had a lot of film-editing and story-editing experience, and I felt I was ready. I was ready, all right—for the Army. The war came along, and for four years and three months I was "in."

Everything changed. For one thing, I advanced from my twenties to my thirties. Nobody kept a job open for me, and I couldn't see returning to Hollywood without one. I couldn't see starting all over again. I felt old. But I met a man who had several hundred million dollars—Armand Deutsch, a Sears Roebuck heir. He hadn't been doing anything professionally that he liked, so I lighted a fire under him. "Why don't we form a movie company? We'll make films. I'll be the producer and you'll be president and we'll make pictures independently." (Incidentally, during the final two years of the war I was based in Astoria, Long Island, making propaganda films. I couldn't live on my army pay. I was a lieutenant, and living in New York, and trying to do this on that money was impossible. They allowed us to write on the side, if we wanted to, so I began to collaborate with Don Ettlinger on a radio show titled *The FBI in Peace and War*. We wrote eighteen of those things for good money, and it got us by.)

Our first motion picture property came about through a weird fluke. The novel *This Side of Innocence* had been a best seller for a year. Every studio was bidding for it; in reality it was nothing but a potboiler, a triangle story that would have been great for Clark Gable, Vivien Leigh, and Olivia de Havilland. I went to the agent handling the book, Annie Laurie Williams (whom I'd known slightly from earlier days), and said, "I want the book." She said, "But

MGM and Fox are bidding; I can't sell this book to you." I said, "Why not? I've got the money; I can write a check for it." (Armand Deutsch could!) She went home that night and looked at her astrological charts and came back in the morning and announced that the charts said I would become an extremely successful movie-maker, and that that she would call me when she decided to sell the book.

So I ended up, an absolute nobody, with Deutsch's money and *This Side of Innocence.*

And at that point every studio in Hollywood came to our doorsteps saying, "Please make it here, we'll finance it, we'll give you . . ." Armand Deutsch, not being experienced in the moviemaking business, began to think, and I can't blame him, "My God, here we are, with the hottest book since the Bible. I can't depend on this young guy who never really made a picture; we've got to get some solidity." The upshot: he fixed on a man named Hal Horne who had worked at one time for a studio as an exploitation and advertising executive, and brought him in, making it a three-way partnership.

The outcome—as you can guess—was voting me out, giving me a settlement. They put $700,000 of overhead developing and exploiting *This Side of Innocence* and never made the picture. (Frankly, it's a story that couldn't be done, now. It's an old-fashioned period piece with lots of ham strutting and posturing, but at the time they could have put that title on a piece of salami and made millions.) So I found myself back in Hollywood with $17,000 settlement money and not a thing to do. But I'd had a foretaste of being an independent producer, and I wanted to become a director, so I decided there was only one thing to do: fix on a property I could option, then get several talented people to work for $50 a week to shape up an independent film company. It was a terribly impractical, illogical idea. But I went at it as though it could work.

I drew from both the Army and from Hollywood. I found five partners—men to whom I literally gave shares in myself. There was a total of one hundred shares. Our lawyer was one partner; he'd negotiated my settlement from Deutsch and Horne. (As a matter of fact, Sam Zagon is still my lawyer.) Sam drew up the company plan.

First we took in George Glass—who is with me right now. George is the most brilliant publicist this business has ever had, in my opinion; we met when he was publicist on *So Ends Our Night*. I said, "How about taking $50 a week, the same as I get and equal shares?" He said, "Great." He's a fighting, bantie rooster type—full of jazz, very bright, with a great concept of what you did with a film, how the line ran to the theater. After George came Carl Foreman, who'd been a sergeant in the Army, also at Astoria, and Herbie Baker who'd had a musical on Broadway when he was twenty-two and in the Army. Sixteen shares apiece.

We took a little office and made big announcements about what we were going to do. One of the first things that happened was a fellow named Willie Shenker coming to see me. Willie's father was in the dress business, and Willie came to me, thinking I was rolling in green stuff, and said, "Look, I want to open a Chinese restaurant in the Valley; my father gave me $7,500 and I need another $7,500." We talked for a while about his restaurant and his money and my company, and to make a long story short I ended up with Willie's $7,500 and he ended up with nine shares of the company. Instead of the restaurant he went to work at Warners in the story department because he couldn't get by on our money.

We took an option on two Ring Lardner stories. One, titled *The Big Town,* we couldn't use because of the radio show with virtually the same name. The other was *Champion.* We decided to adapt *The Big Town,* changing its name to *So This Is New York.* It was high satire, and we starred Henry Morgan, but the film was a colossal bust. We all rolled on the floor when we saw it, but nobody else laughed. I guess there were too many inside jokes. George Glass did a great job promoting it, but nothing could make it work; however, he did keep the pot boiling about the pictures we had "in preparation."

Unfortunately, we had no more pictures in preparation. I knew that Enterprise would never finance us again after our turkey, so the only thing to do, if we wanted to stay in the business, was to get private funds. Fortunately, I met a man who had a son in Hollywood who wanted to work in this business, and I flew to Miami to see him. A beautiful home, sailboats tied up, dinner on the patio with flares and torches, and a beautiful young wife. I'll never forget the way he lit a cigar and sat back and said, "Now, my boy, tell me the story." At this point I had no script, nothing, just the short story *Champion.* He said, "Remember, my boy, I like lots of action in pictures." So I stood on the broadwalk patio which extended over a lagoon and enacted the story of *Champion* as I saw it, complete with the fights, the dramatic scenes, and the broads. Not a goddam word I said or gesture I made ended up in the film, by the way. I could tell, when I finished, that he liked it, and that if his son worked on it as associate producer he'd give me the money I needed. This is the way it turned out; he put up all the money, about $580,000. And we made *Champion.*

The picture was released, and the rest is history of a sort. It was written brilliantly, I think, by Carl Foreman, and was well directed by Robson, and the publicity by George Glass was magnificent. I'll never forget the figure of Kirk Douglas standing bare to the waist, with the line, "Fighting or loving, he was The Champion." (I must have been a miserable character as far as my directors were concerned, in those days. I was frustrated because I was the producer, promoting the money and casting, putting the package together, and altogether too busy to direct, which was what I wanted to do most of all. But still, there was excitement —starting an independent and making it work. The other independents, like Goldwyn and Disney, may not have been enormous studios, but they were prewar babies and established, and we were postwar babies who weren't even founded on a solid basis.)

After *Champion* we had the idea of switching *Home of the Brave* from a Jewish problem story into the Negro vernacular. It took only three weeks to write the whole picture because we simply took the entire play, added one sequence, and kept our switch consistent. It turned out magnificently, and did very well at the box office.

At this time let's not forget Willie Shenker, who gave up his Chinese restaurant. With his shares of the company he eventually opened one of the best damned Chinese restaurants in the world, out in the Valley where he'd originally planned. Only instead of $7,500 he ended up with over $120,000.

After *Home of the Brave,* we made *Cyrano de Bergerac* which didn't make any money at all, even though José Ferrer won the Oscar for his performance. And *The Men,* another loser. Then we hit again, with *High Noon. High Noon* was very successful for its time. It gross doesn't mean much, nowadays, but it kept United Artists going at the time it came out. Between profits and losses, the men in the company weren't really making any money to speak of and still were working damned hard. We were making one film per year, and I wasn't getting my kicks out of it because I wasn't directing. But everyone began screaming so hard to start making money that I gave in, and we made a deal with Columbia to produce five pictures per year, with the idea of parceling out production opportunities to all who wanted it, so they could advance their careers. (I still had no screen credits at that time. I was "Executive Producer," a sort of Zanuck, j.g.)

Well, the pictures we made were interesting as far as subjects were concerned, and we brought in some young, talented people, but the whole goddam thing was a fiasco. We did *My Six Convicts, Death of a Salesman, The Happy Time, Sniper, The Member of the Wedding, The Juggler*—all terrible, terrible financial disasters. Even *The Fourposter* laid a big egg at the box office. But then I got rights to *The Caine Mutiny,* and with that we bailed out the whole package.

Long before *The Caine Mutiny,* we had disbanded. Glass stayed on longest; he wanted to be a producer, so eventually he made a production deal. Foreman went to England after we bought out his share for $275,000. He's a talented man, and he's been doing very well since.

Another investor who came out well, fortunately, was a lettuce grower in Salinas, Bruce Church. He was a wonderful man—he came out well backing *Cyrano* and *The Men,* and *High Noon.* I still remember him saying, "Well, boy wonder, do you want another hundred thousand?" Lettuce growers like that don't grow on trees.

But after the fiasco at Columbia—redeemed, for the

greater part, by *The Caine Mutiny*—I was alone. All my original partners had left, at one time or another, for one reason or another. Perhaps this is precisely as it should have been, because I hadn't been that happy as a producer running the show. Always, during those years, I regretted not directing.

What to do next? I went back to United Artist to see Max Youngstein, and said, "Max, I'd love to come back to U.A. as an independent, financed by U.A., but I have to direct my own pictures. I haven't 'officially' directed, yet, but I know how. Can you help me?" He fronted for me, and they let me do a film. It was *Not as a Stranger,* a potboiler, but very successful financially. Sinatra, Mitchum, Brod Crawford, and Olivia de Havilland starred. It wasn't top-drawer film-making, but it was top drawer commercially, and it set me up as a director.

Since that time I've never had to relinquish my independence. Some of my pictures have been highly successful, some highly unsuccessful. The mistakes I've made and the victories I've gained have been on an independent basis, which is as it should be. The only frustration, now that I am a director, is that I always feel I should be doing better work. While it's true that I control a film (particularly as producer-director) many people contribute to the film, and it's never exactly as I see it. The violins are never as you imagined them to be. The lighting isn't precisely what you had in mind before the film was shot. Things may be better, sometimes, but still they're never quite as you thought they should be. But here in Hollywood you spend such magnificent sums of money for one day's work that if it isn't precisely right you make some settlement, some compromise, because logic doesn't allow you to spend an extra $36,000 to make some thing just a tiny bit better. Consequently, at the same time that I've enjoyed, and luxuriated in, and taken advantage of, my status, I've tried to be as honest as I can in terms of giving of myself and being responsible to all the people who have money flowing into the film.

There simply is no rationale to the amount of money which is necessary to produce a film in Hollywood. This is why the foreign film-maker has us straddled, in a way. We can get exorbitant returns from *Sound of Music* or the James Bond sort of thing, but they're the exceptions. They're extraordinary. But every other film we make has an uphill battle, simply because it costs so much to make them—whether they're good or bad, elaborate or simple. They have to gross an unreasonable amount of money to break even, and if they don't make it the people involved can expire right along with them. It costs too much to make, to distribute, to publicize, to exhibit films from Hollywood.

The producer—who is the last one to get his money back—is the one who rides the highest or, more often, falls the hardest. If a film breaks even the distributor gets his money, and the theater operator gets his cut, but the producer starts making money after everyone else has shown a profit. I think certain adjustments are going to have to be made out here, if we are to exist on a competitive basis.

I also believe that we are given too little credit for some truly wonderful pictures we do produce. Everywhere else in the world film-making is called an art; here we call it an industry. And against our economic odds we frequently create a picture which is truly a work of art. It isn't easy, but it is done more often than critics admit.

I use the term "economic odds" advisedly. Take the best foreign film of any given year, say *A Man and a Woman*. Its gross is very large in relation to its costs, but if we made that same film here that gross wouldn't even let us break even. They make a fortune; we'd lose our shirts.

I also feel—and I have to say this carefully—that what they do is somehow easier than what we do. If I could, at their cost, give full expression to my imagination and creative urges, limited by the extent of my talent, I believe I would do more than they do. They're not even limited by form, but we must tell a story which has a beginning, a middle, and an end, that must capture the responses of a mass audience—if we're to stay in business.

To me, the ability to tell a story on film remains the greatest element of artistry in the medium. To tell a story, and tell it simply and effectively is a great challenge. Are we outdated or sterile or reactionary in being wedded, as we are, to the story? I don't think so. It does not follow that to be outrageous is to be necessarily good.

Often I ask myself, "What is it with me? What do I believe? What do I want? What do I think I want?" There are no easy answers. I don't know if it's the gradual hardening of my arteries, or my own indecision, that leads me to say, "After all this time, I really don't know what I want." If you could wave a wand and say, "Go anywhere in the world and make any film you want to make, under any circumstances," I'm not sure of where the hell I'd go or what the hell I'd do. I'm not absolutely positive that making films would be the first desire because I've reached the point where the hub of my universe is not necessarily picture-making. I have a feeling for it, but not in the way I've been doing it. (Would I want to work like Fellini? I don't know.) I do know that I want to spend less time with all those things which have no direct relationship to what appears on the screen, I think that anyone who makes a film here spends one hell of a lot of time on its financing, budgets, overhead, distribution, selling—all the things I am involved with—through necessity.

I've gone through the stages of my career after some defeats. Once I thought the living end would be to make a great deal of money. I've never done this, but perhaps now, if I make a great deal of money, I can afford to be at the university for two years as an outlet. But I'm not sure that even at UCLA I'd find enough students who were talented to make it worthwhile. I get a charge from younger people, but I think every teacher must eventually wonder if it's worth it. But people say, "What do you mean, you haven't made money?" Sure, the chunks of income sound good. But the way things work out here, with the superchargers and retroactives and surcharges, and all the haggling of financing, I've usually deferred my salary or waived a percentage. True, I have a cult of my own. I'm not sure how I acquired it; I think mine is from the European, the foreign in general, and it's substantial. But strangely enough, many of the foreign film-makers feel exactly the same way about what they're doing as I do about what I'm doing. Many would like to come here to make a film, and some of them have. Is it that the grass is always greener, or is there a profound difference?

I could make one film per year, conveniently, if I didn't have all the details of a company with which to deal. I leave the company to stay independent, and the independence is something I'd not easily give up. Even if I wanted to do a story very, very badly, and had to do it as a director with someone else producing, I don't think I'd do it. Not any more. Perhaps then I'd decide it was time to sit down and do what everyone else does; write it.

But even the idea of writing a book doesn't make any sense. I haven't come to any conclusions. I don't know how I could have come through all these years and not have arrived at certain conclusions—about what the industry ought to be, what it isn't, and why it isn't. Perhaps it isn't meant to be. We are that strange two-headed monster here: the industry which aspires to be an art. And we really can't be both. The whole crusade is glorious, but eventually all the beautiful apples are tainted by the rotten one hidden below, and it all becomes industrial, finally, no matter what is attempted.

The exception is so remarkable. I bow from the waist in utter awe when it happens here.

At a point when *Guess Who's Coming to Dinner* was in production, Stanley Kramer spoke of the personalities who dominated it and the shape the movie had taken.

STANLEY KRAMER: *Guess Who's Coming to Dinner* is almost totally unusual in terms of the Hollywood scene today, including its inception. There aren't many original stories being written for the screen in Hollywood anymore. William Rose, who wrote this original, is probably the most remarkable and, in my opinion, the most talented writer in the original story field. He came to me several years ago with *It's a Mad, Mad, Mad, Mad World,* also an original. We worked together on that one, however, to a far greater extent than I intruded into *Guess Who's Coming to Dinner.*

The idea for this film was his from the beginning—the idea of a sophisticated girl inviting a young Negro, wth whom she had become enamored, home to dinner with her family. Rose also conceived of the family as being rather liberal, because the picture would not be amusing and pressured to the same extent if they weren't people who lived a progressive life in terms of the society in which we exist.

This is where we started. I suppose additional development came out of a series of walks we took through Beverly Hills at night, and a lot of meetings at the Beverly Wilshire Hotel drugstore, and in his studio on the Isle of Jersey where Rose lives. Certainly he picked everything he could from everyone with whom he came in contact. The picture simply grew. He developed the character of the Catholic Monsignor, and the parents of the Negro doctor, who weren't in the original concept but came out of discussions. A remarkable addition was the Negro maid who, as part of the household for many years, is accorded certain privileges. These interrelationships began to generate power and direction.

Rose left with most of the story and the characters in mind and went back to Jersey. I flew there a few months later, and we discussed the project to the point he'd reached. We made additions and deletions, then he went to work with a vengeance. I presume the most important thing we both realized, in those early days, was that the picture would be a humorous examination of a ludicrous situation. It dared be humorous about a story which had a very serious base, and it could only be done this way. This takes, as you might imagine, a tremendously talented and innovative writer, and I think he's pulled it off. We started with the idea that the film should cover two or three days, and wound up with confining it to twelve hours, to keep the compulsion at a boil.

From the beginning I dealt with the story in terms of the actors I felt simply had to do it. Rose agreed with me; only Tracy and Hepburn and Poitier would be acceptable to us in terms of handling this material—

handling it as we felt it had to be done. Obviously, a lot of other people could have played the parts, but only these three could act and react in terms of the story and characters we had in mind.

As a result I talked to Tracy and Hepburn and Poitier even before we had a line on paper. I simply told them the dream of it, the roughest of concepts, and they were all terribly excited but wondered if the dream could be set down. I ad-libbed scenes to them (many of which were dropped as Rose developed the script), and finally all three of them were signed, sealed, and delivered, long before the script was finished. I suppose they could have balked and refused to do it if such-and-such scenes weren't rewritten, or whatever; but no such thing happened.

This was one of the few instances where the blend of actors and material was ideal from the point of concept. Few changes were made in the final script. We certainly met with them to discuss possible changes—with Tracy and Hepburn separately, and then together, and with Poitier in New York. We discussed scenes where perhaps this person should be less or more aggressive, and so forth, and made slight modifications, but no great changes were required.

At this juncture—a bit past the midway point—I talked to Stanley Kramer about his attitudes toward the film and his estimation of the stars.

STANLEY KRAMER: It feels good enough, at this stage of shooting, to keep me up at night. This isn't unique, and it isn't something peculiar to me. I think that anybody who becomes involved and deeply enmeshed in trying to maintain a whole situation from beginning to end must go to sleep and wake up and reexamine what happened during the day. "Oh, the way I let her read that line. It's too loud, too brass, too blatant. Why didn't I have her turn away at that point?"

I'm plagued with this sort of thing all the time. They are perpetual little frustrations. But finally, if they get to be more than little frustrations, I do the scene over again. I've never made formal retakes, you know. I've always included everything that I do throughout the process of shooting. If something is wrong I'm bothered by knowing that it's even in the can, and I won't let the cutter put it in the first assembly until I've done it again.

But who in this business is ever totally satisfied?

Take a scene we did last week, the close-up of Spencer Tracy when Poitier first tells him he is going to marry his daughter. Poitier says he is sorry that Tracy is hearing it this way, that they thought there might be a way they could break the news to him gently. The first time I shot it Tracy stood, and for some reason or other it looked as though he took the shock too seriously. So I did it over and had him sit down because the shock must be almost in the vernacular of the clown. The character who is accustomed to being blatant and forthright suddenly has the ground cut out from under him; his mouth is almost hanging open as a result of the shock. It's hilarious when Tracy does it this way, perhaps the most hilarious scene in the picture. It was good the way we did it the first time, too, but so much better the second. This is an afterthought, drawn from going over the material.

Tracy is the heavy seven-eighths of the way through the picture. He's a wonderful and delightful heavy, but he's the one who says. "What the hell is going on here? Who do they think they are? Who does that man think he is? I'm not going to agree to this. They're not going to rush me." He's the heavy, but he's the one with whom we identify. This is why it is so important to have Spencer Tracy in the part. Because when he switches he may not switch anybody with him, but he certainly will give a lot of people something to think about.

Now, as to the stars—if anything, I feel stronger about all of them than I did before we started production, if that's possible. Remember, we're talking about the very best, to begin with.

Spencer Tracy is the world of the motion picture; neither limited by it nor confined to it. He *is* the motion picture. Spencer Tracy as an actor, in terms of technique or of projecting the actor—what is going on in his mind, by way of face and body—simply has no peer. He is the finality, to me the living end.

I came to Spencer Tracy late in his career, perhaps not so early in mine. I had done three films with him—*Inherit the Wind, Judgment at Nuremberg* and *Mad, Mad, Mad, Mad World*. During *Mad World* he was really quite ill, and I felt that he had to drive himself just to do it. Perhaps his level of irascibility and his stamina may be lower than they were before, but I didn't know him before. He has a range, now, which I call ten to four—ten in the morning to four in the afternoon. This is selfish on my part, because I'm anxious to nurture and husband his strength and power, perhaps to an extent that goes overboard. But five hours with Spencer Tracy is better than eight hours with most other actors.

I would be willing to say, if someone asked me, "You've made films; what do you remember best? What do you hold most dear?"

"The moment I came into the orbit of Spencer Tracy and watched him react to someone else's lines."

Tracy and I have always felt a certain rapport; on

my part, an affection and respect which is almost sticky, certainly overly sentimental. If I have a major sentiment it is in regard to Spencer Tracy, because I've never come in contact with anyone like him since I've been in the making of films.

What can I say about Katharine Hepburn? She is a legend in her way as Tracy is in his; immediately after picturing Tracy in one role I thought of Katharine, because she seemed one of the two or three actresses who could do the part as we saw it. After you got by Hepburn, and perhaps Vivien Leigh, came a big drop in the quality of choice. But if Kate liked it, and could see her way through it, the teaming was great.

Katharine is very selective, you know; I think she needs to express herself in a movie, or in the theater, or whatever, but that she has long since passed the point where just to work, just to do a job, is satisfactory. There has to be something in it.

The same thing is true, in a different way, about Tracy. I think he would have to want to do something very badly to tackle it. Therefore, the fact that they're doing it, means that they see some of the magic Rose and I found in the overall idea. This is an initial vindication, as it were.

Katharine Hepburn is the most completely thorough, driving, constantly-seeking actress with whom I've ever been associated. By this I mean that she's never really satisfied; she never stops thinking about what she's doing and about what everybody else is doing. She mingles, meddles, and intrudes into everything.

When she signed for the film she said, "I bet I'll bug you; I bet I'll drive you crazy." I said, "I bet you will, too, and I'll tell you how we'll live with it. If we both really understand the project and want the film to be very good, then you go ahead and bug me, drive me crazy. I'll let you know, but don't stop doing it."

Katie always comes up with something creative. She's not always right, in my opinion, but she's right 60 percent of the time. What she comes up with adds to and enriches; it's a beautifully-conceived contribution. If I am merely willing to keep my mind open enough to think, "This isn't an intrusion, it's a contribution, and a major one," I never have any difficulty.

As a result I have gotten along with her famously, and I'm sure she respects me because I respect her. When I say, "You ought to take that damned bow off your shoulder," she looks at it, thinks about it, and says, "Why?" If I have a good reason she usually takes it off. And if she says to me, "If I stood with my back to her in this scene it would be more effective than facing her," I think about that. (I've spent a lot of time staging that scene; I've got it to a point where I think it's pretty good, but if I have enough perspective to see that she's right—wonderful.)

Katie contributes to everything. She's got something to say about the words, about the costumes, the camera angle, the lighting, the camera man, the dress designer, everything. She is total. She examines everything, every minute detail. The ashtrays on the tables, the way a lamp is connected and where. (She claims that in her house a wire would never show, so in our picture the wires don't show.)

She is a marvelous woman who has a capacity for many emotional areas, and she has a great talent. She can trigger an emotional truth at precisely the right time. I don't know what she draws on; it's a deep, deep well. Not only does she go to the well for each take, but she reaches down to varying levels, and says, "Let me know if you want a little more or a little less." The word, the only word, for Katie is "magnificent."

Now, Sidney Poitier. Sidney and I were associated once before in *The Defiant Ones,* which was a successful venture. (Now, what the hell does "a successful venture" mean? That it turned out well? No film ever turns out as well as you'd like it to. Does it mean that it was economically successful at the box office? It was, considering the subject. It delved into a field which, theoretically, is not supposed to be a bonanza, a great hit with the mass audience. So I guess we succeeded.)

At any rate, I know Sidney well; perhaps you come to know anybody with whom you do a film well. As a matter of fact it's only when you work with someone from both sides of the camera that you really know their capabilities; you can admire an actor in a film, but not until you work with him do you know just how much of a contribution that actor made or is capable of making. So many people are involved, from writer to director to cameraman to actor, that the actor's contribution is unknown unless you, yourself, have worked on the film.

At any rate, I knew Sidney, and felt that he hadn't even scratched the surface, that he was capable of going in so many directions. But with this film it wasn't a question of his status as a star, of his being Poitier, but the conviction that he was *the* Negro actor for this role. I knew it was something he would understand, intellectually, and that he would be very helpful in other ways, since he would understand the ground on which he would tread.

(I did not assume that *Guess Who's Coming to Dinner* would present the total truth. But I don't think there is a total truth. You find part of it, and believe as you wish, but it is entirely possible to build the biggest lie in the world on a partial truth.)

I met Sidney in a tearoom in New York one wintry day and poured out everything, not necessarily in context. I told him what the dream was, what we were doing, and I said, "Look, the revolution is only a backdrop with a thing like this. This is an inventive comedy, an inventive entertainment of our times, for our times. The people in this picture are not unpleasant people. This does not mean that they are not caught in a web of circumstance and that the crunch is not there; it merely means that they are quite normal people who are not necessarily in the forefront of the issues. They are, themselves, caught in the web of the issue and react as people do with humor and pathos, with as much understanding or lack of understanding as normal people would react; out of this dramatic pressure comes humor.

"In other words, it isn't necessarily humorous when a father doesn't like either the boy or the family of the boy his daughter brings home as a fiancé. Yet his reactions *can* be funny. They can also be poignant and touching and dramatic. Losing a daughter and gaining a son is one of the timeless basic situations."

Here I approached Sidney, a man who has a great deal of responsibility in regard to this revolution, who represents a great deal. I'm not sure Sidney, himself, realizes how much he does represent, though I think he's more aware of his position now then he has been. I watch Sidney, and it's touching to see Negroes who are sweeping the floor or driving a truck, Negroes limited to menial jobs through lack of education through no fault of their own, come up to Sidney and get a wonderful sort of glow. I don't necessarily find this unsentimental, and I'm not referring to total truth again, but it's touching; from Sidney they get a feeling that one of their fellows made it. He's an influence and an inspiration, just because he is what he is. I frankly think Sidney would be where he is if he were white, green, pink, or yellow, but it just happens he's a Negro and has made it against so many odds. Jackie Robinson made it first in *his* field and became something special; Sidney has become this for the same reason. He wears this hat lightly. He's realistic about it because he's extremely intelligent as well as talented. So to come to Sidney with this idea, this dream, is an approach based upon modesty and respect, because no matter what feelings I have in my heart, no matter how Rose and I have fitted together our concept, I now come to Sidney, the point where the hair is really short, and I say:

"Look, we want to do this to turn some light on the sphere of the times. We want to turn the sphere a little and let some sunlight fall on a certain part of it. Will you play this part? Are you willing to take the position and prestige which you so securely have and come with us because you react to it? Do you think it's right?"

He being Sidney Poitier, the answer was an unequivocal, "Of course; my God, it's beautiful."

The only thing we can say in the face of so much racial violence and tension is to ask people to approach this one facet, to sit through it, dip into it, react positively or negatively, love it or hate it, but look at it to see if it can amuse you. You may have heard of someone in this situation, or you may be in this situation. What would you do? How would you react?

Sidney's only qualification was to want to make sure that certain things could be set down, and that the right people would play the other parts. Now I must admit that I returned to my earlier days, when I had to promote money for my films—the parlaying. I told Sidney I had Hepburn and Tracy before I actually had them signed, and I told Hepburn and Tracy that I had Sidney before I had him signed. But they all came together, and that is what mattered.

Sidney has a greatness and professionalism and a deep, deep sensitivity. I have a feeling that Sidney is going to change the course of his career soon, and do a great deal of directing. I have a feeling that he will never be as satisfied as an actor as he deserves to be, if only because there are only so many leading roles he can play as a Negro. A white actor with only half as much talent as Sidney has can get a choice part or two every year, but unfortunately Sidney can't whitewash himself (God knows he wouldn't want to) or pretend to be white. He's an absolutely beautiful man, inside and out, but the fact remains that he's a Negro in an industry that doesn't exactly overflow with great parts for great Negro actors. I'm sure Sidney recognizes this as a limitation, and that direction, or direction and production, for the theater and the motion picture, must be a possibility.

As I said, when I talk about these three [Tracy, Hepburn, and Poitier], I'm starting with perfection.

Strangely enough, Hepburn's niece got into the act only indirectly through Miss Hepburn. I started looking for a girl to play opposite Poitier, and I felt that since Poitier was a major established personality that I didn't want to use an established actress. I wanted a new girl, an actress not really known, consequently more convincing playing opposite Poitier. It seems to me that a known white actress playing opposite Sidney would not be as real.

When I first came into contact with Katharine Houghton I didn't know she was Katharine Hepburn's niece. I saw her in a Garson Kanin play (I don't even remember its name, now). She had a small part, but she impressed me. At the time Carl Reiner was doing a film at Columbia, and in the film he needed a girl who could play a Jewish girl from New York. Katharine Houghton is many miles from that, but Carl interviewed her, and read her. Then Carl heard that I was looking for a girl, and he told me that Katharine Houghton was completely wrong for what he was doing, but that she really had it as an actress and if she photographed well she'd be sensational. Then he said, "Incidentially, you know, she's Katharine Hepburn's niece." I made a note of this, but didn't do anything because I planned to go to New York soon and see many young actresses. But a week later Hepburn called me and said, "You must see my niece." I said, "You mean Katharine Houghton?" She was surprised but said, "Yes." I said, "I'll see her when I go to New York." Katie said, "But when are you going to New York? You'll cast the part without seeing my niece." I said, "No, I'll wait until I go to New York before I cast that part. After all, I don't have you absolutely cast, yet, and I don't want to end up with your niece and not you." She thought this was funny, and she said, "Well, I'm going to tell her to see you in New York."

I went, I saw her, and I was completely intrigued. I didn't know whether she could act or not, but I spent about two and a half hours talking to her, and told her I'd come back to New York in about ten days and have her read. This we did. I came back to Hollywood, told Katie that Miss Houghton was a possibility, returned to New York and read with her for about three hours. She just read all the parts in the script, the first draft I had. I didn't ask her to do this; she just read, right from the beginning, all the parts. And I said, "I think you'll do just great with this part," and that's how she was cast. She never made a screen test.

Now everything—script and stars—had passed into my hands for translation. Bringing together all the elements was like being in a room with a lot of balloons suspended against the ceiling, their strings hanging down. Could all the strings be gathered in one hand so that the balloons could be pulled together? I had to act confident, to say, "I am confident."

I've never lacked confidence, even when I was atrociously wrong; I've been like the punch-drunk fighter who gets hit hard, knocked out, but approaches the next fight feeling he's going to murder the bum.

If you don't have confidence, how are you going to do anything? Especially make a movie? How are you going to overcome the objections of the distribution company, or the people who finance it, or the people who advertise the film, or the exhibitors, if you don't say, "Wait a minute—this is the greatest thing since the coming of Christ." You exploit yourself. You overdramatize what you're doing. And when people come to see it and decide it doesn't live up to what I've promised, they're disappointed—which is one of the shortcomings of my approach, and a wholly different story.

But to do *Judgment at Nuremberg* or *The Defiant Ones* or *On the Beach* or even *Ship of Fools* I had to generate so much in advance with the people who were going to finance and sell just so I could *make* the pictures, that things were bound to fall below expectations. Some were wrongly cast; sometimes, just to make the film, I'd say, "All right, I'll put Joe Zilch in it." I didn't want to put in Joe Zilch, but I had to, in order to make the film in this economic climate in which I live. Sometimes I haven't even made it go; sometimes I've abandoned films I wanted desperately to do.

I just got through abandoning one. I developed, with Abby Mann, a magnificent piece of material titled *Andersonville*. I brought it up to the starting line after working on it for a year and a half. At that starting line, Columbia, which was having financial stricture or was involved in a change of hands, didn't have the money to make a six or seven million dollar film, so I had to let it go and do something else.

One can't prove what will transcend the barrier in terms of public acceptance until you make the picture. Then, if they accept it, something wondrous happens. I'll admit that the wondrous thing doesn't happen too often. If you do something a little special it has to be extraordinary before they jump the barrier to receive it.

I think *Guess Who's Coming to Dinner* is special—perhaps the most special film I've ever developed. And if it isn't really top drawer, if it doesn't accomplish 100 percent what we have in mind, I won't jump the barrier.

It simply has to be a film that people, whatever other reactions they might have, will talk about—will say, "Oh, you've got to see it, it's hilarious," or, "You've never seen anything like it!" or "She's simply wonderful!" This is a hell of an intimidating way to start a film. I've started this way before, and I've fallen short, and the pain is a kind of pain that starts somewhere near the groin and goes up to the chest, as though you're having a heart attack in the stomach. It's a terrible pain when a picture is rejected and people don't come to see it. I've had the experience so often that the pain softened my aggressions. I'm afraid it's happened as often to me as to anyone in the business.

Going back to films I produced and/or directed—*The Men, Cyrano, Member of the Wedding, Inherit the Wind, Ship of Fools.* Films of that caliber (and there were many others less successful) can just fail, and you know that the failure isn't keyed to a performance. The chemistry of the film simply couldn't entice the audience. That great amorphous mass is lined up across the street, responding chemically to another film, and they're ignoring yours totally. What is this chemistry, the pursuit of the rainbow? You say, "Oh, James Bond," so you make eighty of them, but by the time the seventy-ninth comes along they're rejecting that, too. But a film that aspires to be something special, something not blatantly sexual or violent, can only succeed when the final ball of wax is warm, soft, translucent, exciting, attractive.

I'm afraid that my feelings about films which get a "Good try, old boy," are definitely anti. Only making it is important, and I mean "making it" at the box office. I've heard God knows how many conversations about "breaking ground," but you don't break anything with a film which people don't see and respond to in sufficient numbers. Perhaps you suggest, through your failure, a way in which another film-maker might succeed, but you haven't done anything yourself. You've made a contribution, perhaps; but I can't satisfy myself with the rationalization or the excuse that "My film was ahead of its time," because I don't believe that. I don't believe that anything is ahead of its time if you do it right.

My God, you get so self-centered talking about yourself, particularly in a long spurt like this, that you become entranced with the tinkling sound of your own voice, as though your philosophy is one of the most important things in the world. And only in a tiny sense does it matter. I remember when I attended the Moscow Film Festival. They request that the person associated with a film that is shown get up to say something about the film. One producer—I think he was from Norway—got up and said, very simply, "I'm happy at being introduced and I'm grateful for the warmth with which you receive me, but what is there for me to say? You're about to see my film, and either *that* says it or we're wasting our time." I was impressed by this.

My feeling is that over a period of years you don't know where you belong in the firmament, if you belong in the firmament at all. I look at my whole body of work, of all varieties, dealing with all the themes I've touched, and I frankly think, without mock humility, "Well, because this was where it was, because it was Hollywood incarnate, and I was making an assault upon what (for want of better terminology) we'll call the 'Establishment' of my time, working with subject matter rather than art, that the subject matter dominated the art. I never got enough inner satisfaction from the creation of it because the creation was dominated just by the fact of its coming into existence, so I'll have to find the satisfaction elsewhere." I haven't found it yet.

It hasn't been a question of success. I have had films which made money; I've made more which have lost money. But I haven't found the real satisfaction I want, as yet, and maybe I never will. I've never thought, about any of my films, "This is the best concept I could have managed." But I always say, "The next one will be."

I'm saying, now, that *Guess Who's Coming to Dinner* will be.

In a final session with Stanley Kramer, I asked him about the fairly well-publicized period at Columbia when his production unit operated under the heavy thumb of Harry Cohn.

STANLEY KRAMER: I didn't exactly have much of an association with Cohn. What happened was that I made a deal with Cohn I never should have made. It wasn't his fault. I made a deal with him for multiple films because I had an organization and everybody within the organization wanted to be doing something; producing, directing, writing, whatever.

The deal I made was to supervise the production of ten pictures simultaneously, something I not only didn't want to do but didn't feel I could do. So the fault is mine.

My contract stated that he would have no control over the films I made but that his company would have all the the control over the distribution of those films. As a result he came to dislike and resent me because, I think, he thought of me for awhile, as a potential heir apparent—and that was the last thing I wanted to be. I never wanted to run a studio, and I never will; the idea is anathema to me. But he suspected it was what I wanted, and I knew this, so as a result I kept pulling away from him. I was afraid to go to the dining room and talk to him, so I never went, and he considered that a big snub. I never went to his home, and he considered that a big snub. So he became determined to turn the whole situation into a total failure, which it became. And he didn't make it a failure; I did.

My whole relationship with him was a fiasco. Designed and created and screwed up and executed by me, as though I built a gallows and hung myself. I was in a place I didn't belong, doing what I shouldn't be doing, and not doing it well. In fact, had it not been for *The Caine Mutiny* it would not only have been a fiasco, it would have been a major tragedy. *The Caine Mutiny* pulled all the chestnuts out of the fire. It was the last picture I made for Cohn. (Ironically, it was from Harry Cohn I wangled the right to buy and make *The Caine Mutiny,* so even at this point I have no complaint against him.)

Yet he was a cruel man. He was cruel to many, many people. In the final analysis he was cruel to me for my steadfastness in resisting him, and for my own inner arrogance in the creative function. From the heir apparent (which I didn't agree to and didn't really know about), I turned into the enemy. So he decided to expunge me, which he did, very satisfactorily.

But when I was through there, having finished *The Caine Mutiny,* I found that I owed him a great deal. He really made me a director. He did it indirectly, but after failing with everything but *Mutiny* (the other pictures weren't all bad, incidentally, but they didn't even make money, and Columbia didn't even bother to distribute them properly), I was both strong enough and humble enough to wangle a deal to direct, which was what I'd wanted to do in the first place. He turned me into an all-the-way gambler, into the producer-director I am now. He drove me to what I really wanted.

On the whole I think the passing of the tycoon types, the Mayers and Warners and Cohns, has been good for the industry. These men served well in their time. They were wizards of a realm unknown to those who are making films today. They were industrial wizards in an industrial time. When MGM made fifty films a year they had a meeting at the beginning of the year when they said, "All right, we'll make two with Garbo, three with Crawford, two with Montgomery, four with Gable, three with Tracy, two with Shearer." They arbitrarily set things up that way, then found the stories to fit the pattern. It was an industrial situation and it worked. All the films did well. The trade was aggressive, glamorous, exciting—far different from what it is today. About the merchandise, Mayer and Warner and Cohn knew very little; about the merchandising, they knew very much. If you were to sit down and discuss with those people what the motivation for a character in a story might be, you'd end up shaking with fright. That's why so many sensitive people, writers and directors sometimes actors, objected. But, by God, they merchandised.

There might, there just might, be a great and wonderful change coming as a result of their passing. Maybe we won't have as great an industrial combine (though television is taking good care of that), but it's possible that the American film will finally become a great, creative thing. It can't on the present economic operating basis, but the production of television films may fill the studios so thoroughly, they'll cut our tremendous overhead. The films may depend only upon what they are, not a means of supporting all the executive overhead and the sound stages.

I'm terribly interested that there be an atmosphere in which people who like to make films and are interested in making them feel that they can do their best work —without shortcuts, without compromises, without being costed to death. Film-making is like a disease, a real disease. Call it the "celluloid disease," if you will. Films bear no final relationship to theater, television, the writing of fiction, radio. Film is incredibly elastic. There are so many things that can be done with it that haven't been done. There are so many things that can be done with a camera that have never been done. Ditto, color. The prospects are so vast that you become perpetually impatient. You can make a film a year, perhaps every year and a half. Will there be enough years for you? You want to do a color picture with two colors, a film shot through twelve filters, truths, distortions. The closest any other creative person can come is the artist who puts something on canvas because he, too, is limited only by imagination. And then there are the delightful, wonderful things that happen by accident and become part of the invention.

And always, will there be the time? The time to work solidly, the time to experiment? The time to plan the ultimate effect, the time to stumble onto it?

George Glass, Stanley Kramer's vice-president and publicity director, was associated with the company at the beginning. Stanley describes him as a "bantie rooster." He is. Small, bright, alert, aggressive, and single-minded—and ready to produce another view of Kramer.

GEORGE GLASS: Our relationship goes way back—beginning, fittingly, with a press-agent stunt. The year, 1940. I worked for an independent praisery which was in charge of promoting a picture titled *So Ends Our Night,* first of the anti-Nazi films. Stanley was the executive assistant to David Lowe-Albert Lewin, producers of the film for United Artists.

I cooked up a stunt, just for the hell of it, that I called a "striptease picket." A girl in the picture named Gerta Rozan, an extremely well-stacked young lady, ostensibly protested too much cutting of her part. She claimed that it was her first motion picture and that all the cutting was unfair to her cinematic debut. Her protest was unique. She began to picket the studio after announcing to the press that she would remove an article of clothing each day until she was parading up and down Lankershim Boulevard in front of the studio with nothing more than skin between her and the cops. This went on for four days, and she was down to black panties and bra (having rehearsed the whole routine in her apartment to achieve maximum effect) and creating the biggest traffic jam ever seen in those parts.

At this point I needed somebody to rush out of the Lowe-Lewin offices, overcoat in hand to be flung around Miss Rozan as she reached for her bra, then carry her inside for a peace confab. I prevailed upon Stanley to do the chore. He waited, red-faced and self-conscious, next to the door. I crouched behind the semiopen door hollering hoarsely to Miss Rozan, "Take it off, take it off!" She was beginning to chicken out, but at last she reached behind her back, and as the bra began to peel away from her adequate white bazoom, out rushed Mr. Kramer with the coat, right on cue, while cameras popped for the edification of millions. Such front-page publicity never before resulted from any movie stunt.

Thus started a firm friendship between us. Stanley admired my brash style. I admired his obvious intelligence, drive, and know-how regarding pictures. We tried, within a year, to get a company of our own going, but we were so short of money we never quite managed. Then came the big war, and Stanley marched off, resplendent in a shavetail's suit, heading for the Signal Corps.

After the war Stanley wanted me to join a company of which he was a part, but I couldn't make it. The deal blew up for him and he came West. We put our heads together again. At the time I was operating my own publicity, public relations, and film exploitation agency, one of the most successful in town. But I folded the shop to throw my future with Kramer. We founded Screenplays, Inc., using that name to emphasize our devotion to the story above all in picture production. Into our company as a junior partner came Carl Foreman, a young writer.

Investors—Stanley told you the story about William

Shenker and the Chinese restaurant. Another investor, as well as coauthor (with Carl Foreman) of our first screenplay, was Herbie Baker, son of the famed stage star and vaudevillian, Belle Baker.

Our first picture, *So This is New York,* starring radio humorist Henry Morgan, was a disaster, through no fault of ours. Certain crises, such as the British ad valorem tax had hit our industry, and we curtailed our budget beyond the point our picture could stand.

During this time I waged an all-out promotional campaign. The sight and sound of our struggles won us lots of friends, especially among the press. This was a factor in our raising the money for our second and third pictures. Stanley proved to be a driving and daring leader and a superb salesman. With the last money we could beg, borrow, or filch, we sent Stanley to Miami to talk to a Midwestern department store magnate with a yen to invest in movies. From this meeting came *Champion* and *Home of the Brave,* both big hits at low budgets.

Champion cost less than $580,000, and *Home of the Brave* about $370,000.

Success came to us at the edge of the precipice. We were all broke. I remember once coming home to find my wife, Harriet, scrubbing the floor on her hands and knees. She had been rolling in servants up to the time we plunged our all into Screenplays, Inc. I had returned from the bank on this occasion to announce that a $400,000 loan was in sight, usable, of course, only for picture-making, not for personal purposes. Harriet's reaction, as she continued her scrubbing, was a baleful look and a sad question: "Great. When do I get up off this goddam floor?"

I recall, most poignantly, that when we got our first profits from *Champion,* Harriet and I decided to do the town. I dusted off my tux and she unwrinkled a long-unworn evening dress. We decided first to sit down and pay our debts, which included sums to a lot of relatives and friends on whom we had placed the bite over a two and one-half year span. At the end of the check-signing, I looked at her and she looked at me. We were so desperately tired that we removed our finery and went straight to bed.

From these two pictures the company skyrocketed. We made movie history of a sort. At the time the entire industry was dispirited. Costs were up. TV was on the horizon. The wartime bubble had burst. People were finding things to do other than going to movies. We were turning out good pictures without too many stars in the cast and at reasonable budgets. On they came. *The Men* for less than $870,000, *Cyrano de Bergerac* at $980,000, and *High Noon* for $890,000. It gave the industry new hope, and lent impetus to independent production. United Artists, through whom these pictures were distributed, gained immense new strength. Imagine, all these pictures together cost less than four million dollars!

Kramer, of course, grew as a film-maker. He was called "the wonder boy." Hollywood loves "wonder boys" and Stanley was the first to lead Hollywood out of the jungle since Irving Thalberg. Company personnel changed, as it seems it always must. Baker dropped out of the setup. Shenker realized more than $120,000 from his $15,000 investment and wound up with The China Trader in the Valley. Stanley and Foreman and I went on. We acquired Sam Katz, the MGM tycoon (and one of the founders of the Balaban and Katz theater chain) as a partner. He led us to Columbia Studios. We were all unhappy there; Columbia wanted us to make six pictures a year. This simply did not suit Stanley's style. And I was unable to give each picture the loving attention our films had always been given. We made some good pictures—*The Wild One* is still an international favorite and the nouvelle vogue forerunner, *My Six Convicts, The Member of the Wedding,* and *The Sniper*. But they were not box-office successes. However, the last big one we made for Columbia, *The Caine Mutiny,* grossed around sixteen million dollars, recouping all the losses and leaving some profits all around.

By this time the strain of the unhappy setup left its effects on the partners. I went my way, Carl Foreman his. Foreman had blossomed under the benign climate into a first-rate screenwriter. He went on to fame under his own steam. I wound up other places, including a stint as exec producer for Marlon Brando's company, Pennebaker.

There are those who say that Stanley and I parted in anger, and I guess this is true, to some extent. Partnerships are like marriages, except that they require more care. You don't have sex as a leavening agent. If you do to your partner what you do to your wife your partnership has had it. But Stanley and I had been through a lot together, and it was rather like sharing a foxhole when the bullets are coming at you. And we always retained a residue of solid friendship, come what may. Through eighteen pictures we had known poverty, fear, ambition, and triumph.

We parted company in 1954, not to become reassociated until this year. Stanley called me and we talked about *Guess Who's Coming to Dinner,* and his next one, *The Secret of Santa Vittoria,* and he asked me to become the v.p., associate producer, and director of publicity for his company. I liked the idea, so here I am, back with Stanley.

I've left out a lot. I'm sure that if I'd ever kept notes the story of our struggle to launch Screenplays,

Inc., would make a great book. We started with less than $25,000, and created a film power that stands today as the Stanley Kramer Company, Inc. It's like taking four bits and parlaying it into a successful railroad.

It is interesting to note that Stanley, on his own, decided to become a film director. He has become one of the best. The industry has recognized his contributions by handing him the Irving G. Thalberg Award. His *Mad, Mad, Mad, Mad World* has grossed thirty million to date for United Artists, one of the largest of all time.

Why a director? Stanley's drive has always been to be the boss, the one who wants things done his way. The time came, in the industry, when directors took greater control over picture-making than they'd ever been able to. So (in my opinion), Stanley decided that's where the action was, consequently where he'd be. I also think he has a natural desire to be recognized as an artist of picture-making, a complete creator. He now has the whole bag: director and producer, both.

Stanley is something of a "loner." You almost have to be to succeed in as many areas of this business as he has. I have never seen anyone match his powers of complete concentration. He plays to win as you would see if you ever watched him damn near kill himself making badminton shots. Loves baseball. Loves sports. Knows a lot about them. He is a fine companion who knows how to relax as completely as he concentrates within his profession.

This is Stanley's twentieth year as a successful independent producer. I don't think he has hit his peak. But his foothills stand a lot higher than the mountains of others in these parts. And I'm happy to be climbing along with him.

Katharine Hepburn

SHE IS a tall woman—five feet, seven and a half inches. She walks with a firm stride. Unless you knew better, she could pass as a truck farmer's wife delivering produce. Her hair is shoved under a cap, but reddish wisps escape from it. The face is weather-marked and ruddy.

The ensemble would shock any reputable couturier. At the throat, a scarf. Below that a GI fatigue jacket, descending to a pair of tan slacks (not tapered), and a heavy pair of shoes that look as though they should be equipped with spikes.

And slung over her left arm a wicker basket that could easily carry four dozen eggs.

But a second glance takes in the cheekbones, the generously wide mouth, the chin. And when she speaks you know that you are in the presence of one of the few truly fascinating women of our time—Katharine Hepburn.

Legends—those based upon personalities—are ephemeral. At the present time the personalities of the entertainment world (where the legend can be most effectively built), who have become legends within a few decades, are few. There is a sad little memory known as Marilyn Monroe; the husky voice and thin face and arched eyebrows of Marlene Dietrich; the full-breasted, determined, overwhelmingly beautiful Elizabeth Taylor; the elusive, forever escaping, Greta Garbo; plus, always, Katharine Hepburn.

When she came into your life depends on your age. There are those who remember her first film, *A Bill of Divorcement,* in 1932 with John Barrymore, her Academy Award-winning performance in *Morning Glory,* and such films as *Little Women* and *Stage Door.* Audiences a decade later start with *The Philadelphia Story* and *Woman of the Year,* as well as *Sea of Grass, Pat and Mike, State of the Union,* and *Keeper of the Flame*—plus three other films, all made with Spencer Tracy. Still another decade later: *The African Queen* (with Humphrey Bogart) and *Summertime.* But actually, your age is unimportant. No matter how over-spattered with commercials televised movies have become, every audience of every age has seen Katharine Hepburn in one performance after another. The depth of interest expressed in this woman is astonishing; as a professional interviewer I have been asked about her more often—perhaps twice as often—than I've been asked about any other other personality.

Oddly enough, the legend of Katharine Hepburn is the result of both her presence and her absence. The constant presence in films shown again and again has already been discussed. But it is her Garbo-like withdrawal from the press, a consuming desire to live privately, that has built the personality the public ultimately loves best—the woman of more shadow than substance, of whom little is known and only slightly more can be assumed. The woman who protects her unique properties—in Miss Hepburn's case a strong talent for both drama and comedy, a distinctive walk and voice, an obvious disregard for Hollywood conventions—is pleasing and bothersome and, above all, intriguing.

After four years of negotiation, during which "no" turned to "maybe," and finally to "yes," she agreed to talk with me extensively about herself, her world, and her life on the set.

The legend that begins with a Katharine Hepburn exposed on the screen and scratched at by the press, is exceeded by only one thing: Katharine Hepburn.

The outfitting as a truck farmer's wife that I described is so consistently worn by Katharine, that I came to regard it as a costume and sought out its origin.

"I found the cap in Germany, between the wars, and I've had it copied over and over again. It was worn by either the German navy or merchant marine, I forget which, but it is practical and chic and it certainly is comfortable. I've even had it copied for this film; I wear it with Jean Louis' military coat all through the earlier scenes.

"My brother left the fatigue jacket behind, once, on a visit, and it's so damned handy, and so perfect for this climate, I've worn it ever since. When it's cold I wear a red sweater beneath it; I've had it forever, and it's going to pieces in back. Moths or time, I don't know which, but I figure it will fall to bits about the same time I do."

The slacks and shoes:

"I'm outdoors a lot. Every morning I take my dog Dog out for a run in the woods at the reservoir. Between the poison oak and brambles I'd be a mess if I didn't protect my legs and feet. Besides, I don't particularly give a damn how I dress. I never have."

The market basket:

"Everything goes into it. Script, any old thing I might need at the studio. I know it looks as though I'm delivering eggs, but it would be the height of stupidity to cram all these things into a purse."

Finally, the ruddiness of her complexion:

"I'm spotted, you know. Freckled. I can't take sun, but I virtually live in the sun. California's the worst place in the world for a complexion like mine; I should at least wear makeup, but I can't stand makeup. I put it on before I go in front of the camera and take it off the minute I walk off the set.

"It's been serious, from time to time. I've had skin cancers removed, including a rather large one, here," she pointed to a spot near her chin, "after *The African Queen.*"

She laughed. "Not very practical, am I?"

The only problem a journalist encounters in spending much of six weeks on and off the set with Katharine Hepburn is one of logistics. Virtually everything she says is quotable. Her range of interests is vast, her mind sharp. Her tongue instinctively produces astute phrasings. She is also endowed with a rich sense of humor, a humor based upon mature and tolerant understanding of the world about her, and (most impressive) upon her own life and career.

One day, between takes, I watched her go through a box of stills. Columbia has given her the right to clear the hundreds of still pictures shot for publicity during the course of the film. As she howled her way through them—approving more than she folded over and cast aside—I asked her about her basis for judgment.

"The camera can be an enemy, even in the kindest hands. My niece is a very intelligent girl, and lovely, but every once in a while one of these shots will make her look like my idiot daughter. Out they go.

"I'm not really vain, but I don't think people want to see the wrinkles on my neck. They're quite unattractive. Nor do they want to see me look like a corpse, or like a monkey. I feel under no obligation. Besides, I like to be gorgeous and this I can control."

The steady visitor to the set quickly noticed Katharine's presence in capacities other than actress. Often Katharine Houghton was involved in scenes apart from her aunt. Yet Hepburn was almost constantly nearby, watching, hunkering down near the camera. Between takes she took Kathy aside, suggesting a different way to deliver a line, the angle at which ankles should be crossed for the camera, the tilt of her face.

"It's really difficult to give advice to someone," she said at one point, "but I can offer a century's worth of experience to Kathy. Fortunately, she's intelligent enough to know what advice she should take and what she should ignore. That's the only value of advice, you know. The person has to know what is good for them and what isn't.

Then, one day, in a scene that involved a rapid dash down a staircase to meet her "mother," Katharine

Houghton took a bad fall, plunging five steps to a tiled foyer, landing on hands and ankles. It was a rather terrible moment, and the crew gasped in fear, for it seemed Kathy must have broken or sprained at least one of her ankles or wrists. Fortunately, the injury was slight. One ankle had been wrenched and became badly swollen and exceedingly painful, but Kathy insisted upon going ahead with the shooting schedule.

I commented on her guts.

"That's when you're grateful to your Anglo-Saxon forebears. Don't make a fuss—get back on the horse. Actually, it's a very odd thing, and perhaps unfortunate, but two of the actresses' greatest assets are love and pain. A great actress, even a good actress, must have plenty of both in her life."

She paused and laughed.

"Poor Kathy. Think of what would have happened if she'd broken something and had to be replaced. After losing this opportunity there'd be just one goddam thing for her to do—kill herself."

Katharine was also on the set when Spencer Tracy was shooting and she wasn't. Again she hunkered near the camera, watching, nodding, sometimes smiling (if things went well in a few takes) or scowling (if she thought Stanley Kramer insisted upon too many). The warmth and affection between these two, born twenty-six years ago with *Woman of the Year*, was obvious. Recently Katharine had helped attend Tracy through an illness in which he twice neared death. Thus her presence during shooting combined the concern felt for a best friend and the tenderness paid a prize patient.

Here, however, she did not do any coaching. Her comments were confined to such remarks as "Isn't he superb!" or "Spencer is the best actor in the world. He is! Total concentration."

There is an oft-quoted story of their first meeting, when Katharine said, "Oh, Mr. Tracy. You aren't nearly as tall as I thought you'd be," and he rejoined, "Don't worry. I'll cut you down to my size."

Neither has cut the other down. The years have only added to their stature.

Guess Who's Coming to Dinner is being filmed thirty-five years after Katharine Hepburn first came to Hollywood. But since all of Katharine's life has been of interest, it seems best to begin the interview rather as we attempted to tape it, from the beginning.

> *Could you trace the vital statistics business—birth, rearing, your entry into your life as an actress?*

KATHARINE HEPBURN: It's very difficult to go back and tell it all. There's so much. My mother and father were, I think, extremely remarkable people. Very much under the influence of Shaw and the Fabian Society. Both had an A.B. and an M.A. Mother was graduated from Bryn Mawr and Radcliffe and Dad from Randolph-Macon and Johns Hopkins. Dad stood very high in his class at medical school until he met Mother, who was teaching school in Baltimore because her sister Edith was studying at Johns Hopkins—quite a thing for a woman to do in those days.

Daddy met Mother when he was fencing with my Aunt Edith. Ma thought, "My God, this is the most beautiful creature I've ever seen." They got married during his last year in medical school, and he plummeted from the top to the bottom of his class in no time at all.

After graduation he didn't want to practice in a big city, so he rather arbitrarily chose Hartford, Connecticut. (My mother's family, the Houghtons, came from Boston and then Corning, New York. My name is Katharine Houghton Hepburn and Kathy's name is Katharine Houghton Hepburn Grant; my mother's, Katharine Martha Houghton. Daddy's family are Virginians, Scottish and Welsh; lots of Powells on his mother's side.)

The Hartford Hospital was a good one, even in those early days. At that time ward operations were performed at the hospital, private ones at home. Daddy went up as an intern; he didn't have a dime, and mother had a little money, and they lived opposite the hospital. When he finished his internship and a residency they got a house that had been built by Charles Dudley Warner, the poet, a man who belonged to the Harriet Beecher Stowe-Mark Lane group.

Our house at 133 Hawthorne Street was brick, painted dark red, with black gingerbread trim and three gables. A charming house, in the most beautiful district of town, with elm trees and big, open lawns, with the houses set very far back. (Warner had written "My Summer in a Garden" there.) The city had actually grown out to this district: next door stood a factory. Once Mother decided that it was terrible for her to have so much property while the poor factory people had to sit on the curb to eat their lunch, so she invited them all in. They scattered papers all over the place, picked the flowers, left an awful litter, and Daddy said, "Now you know the difference between having a philosophy and acting on it."

That was really the difference between Daddy and Mother. She was very left of center, a genuine political philosopher, all-out for the liberation of man and the liberation of woman. The freethinkers used to come and stay at our house, and there was a great deal of conversation. We were always invited to join in, but we never spoke very much; perhaps it was intimidating.

The women of my mother's generation were daring creatures. They were enormously upright, very much freethinkers. Hell, the principles upon which this country was founded were very dear to them, very important. My mother would give way on anything, but she would not give way on certain beliefs. You want this book? Take it. This chair? Take it. Money? Take it. But don't take my thoughts because they're really all I have. (I can remember that when I was first going to go and visit someone on Long Island, I thought I'd have killed myself to travel with the right kind of luggage for the weekend. Now I'd say, what the hell? No bag? Do the stuff up in newspaper. When I get on an airplane I look like a little old lady with all my bundles, and I couldn't care less. I remember when someone gave me some extremely handsome jewelry that was stolen almost immediately; I called Daddy to tell him and he said, "Thank God. You have no right to have that kind of stuff anyway." He was right; he was more or less like Mother in regard to personal possessions.)

My father was an intensely active man. He never took a vacation until he was somewhere in his seventies. He always said, "You must make your life interesting." We used to go on Sunday walks, dragging along anyone who happened to be around, including Sinclair Lewis, of whom we saw a great deal when he lived in Hartford. (And about whom I'll tell you a wonderful story later.) We'd shinny up to the tops of trees and swing them down, and collect wild flowers. There was always a big thing as to who brought back the first trailing arbutus of the season—exquisite flower—and they had to be in bloom. I always found them first; I had a secret spot.

Dad had a great gift with the outdoors, and just taking a walk with him was fun. I think he taught me that I had to make my life interesting, without paying out a lot of money in the process. Doing what offered itself. Accepting challenges. You know, if you say you're going to go a certain distance, climb to the top of a certain thing, don't give up. I was constantly being rescued by my dad from caves and all sorts of things. I was great at getting up, then petrified at the prospect of getting down.

My mother was a true philosopher, in the Greek sense. Life never caused her to be very practical. She always had plenty of money, and she was a genuine political philosopher, enormously well educated. She had a fine mind, a rich sense of humor, and an enormous love for her fellowman. She devoted her life to trying to alleviate the unnecessary agonies of womankind—in getting them the vote, in furthering birth control, and in the great fight against venereal disease. (Both she and Dad were involved in that,) She marched for woman's suffrage, even during the First World War when some people thought it terribly unpatriotic, and she spoke at all the fairs we had around Hartford. I'd be taken along, and I remember being very small and carrying bundles of balloons so big that I almost went up in the air with them.

Dad, I think, was more genuinely artistic. Mother became the most satisfied with me, yet the thing I did that made her the proudest was to deliver the speech that almost ran me out of the business, the speech when I supposedly introduced Wallace [Henry A. Wallace], when I was actually speaking against censorship in the motion picture industry. She was proud, naturally, that I became a success, but she was prouder of that speech, and she used to play the record over and over again. She was very left of center.

On the set with their scripts for *Guess Who's Coming to Dinner.*

Printed in U.S.A.

Katharine Hepburn (left) in her second film, *Morning Glory* (1933); Spencer Tracy and Freddie Bartholomew (below) in scene from *Captains Courageous* (1937).

In *Sea of Grass* (1947) (above) with Edgar Buchanan; in *Adam's Rib* (1949) (left); and in *State of the Union* (1948).

Tracy and Hepburn in one of their first costarring films, *Keeper of the Flame* (1942).

In *Pat and Mike* (1952).

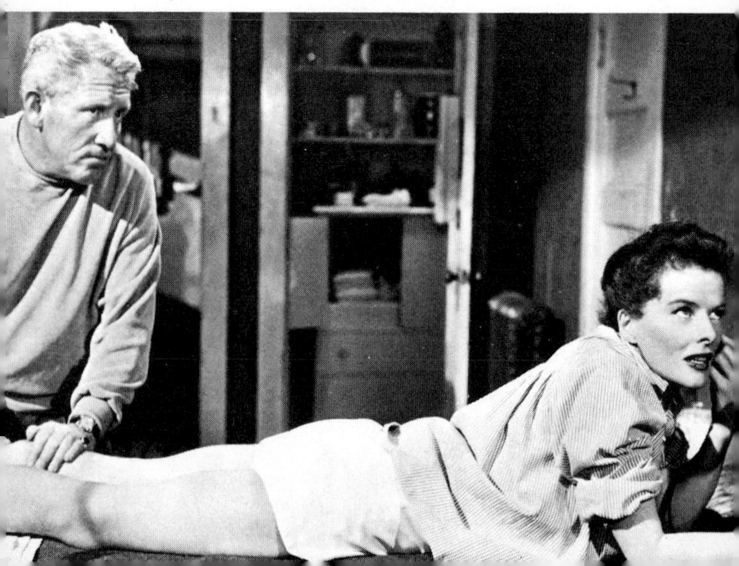

Their last picture together, Hepburn and Tracy in Guess *Who's Coming to Dinner.*

Talking over problems at drive-in.

Cecil Kellaway with Hepburn and Tracy.

Poitier and Tracy (above) having heart-to-heart talk in *Guess Who's Coming to Dinner*. Katharine Hepburn's favorite hat (left)—a cap she found in Germany and had copied many times and wears in this movie.

Family scene from the film.

Katharine Hepburn brushing Tracy's hair before scene is shot.

My mania for physical activity came from Dad. He was a fanatic on that; he felt that when you're soggy physically, you get soggy mentally. I agree with him 100 percent. I polish up my body as best I can. As it gets older it's harder to deal with, and there are certain things you dare not think about at all, but I've got to keep it in as good a shape as I can. I don't talk about it; I just do it. I would die if I didn't exercise every day. I would die if I didn't run. I was out listening to the woodpeckers at 7:30 this morning, before we went into rehearsal. (It's great when I don't have to think of my damned old hair and putting on makeup.) One woodpecker tapped on a hollow telephone pole and the other on a tree, and it was fascinating, like drumbeats in Africa.

Dad could always find a marvelous hill to climb, a view to look at, or something. Lots of fun. I remember that when he was eighty years old I met him in Athens, and when he got off the airplane (he never traveled anything but tourist; he thought I was an absolute ass for wasting my money traveling first class), he said, "Well, let's go and see it." I said, "See what?" and he said, "The Acropolis." I said, "Now, Daddy, you're just off the airplane. You've been in the plane sixteen hours." He said, "Well, I came here to see the Acropolis, didn't I?" and that was that. Up we went.

He had a great capacity to make a game interesting, and life interesting, and an evening interesting, and I think this is a wonderful quality. I have seen too many people who find life an agony, who spend a lot of time analyzing their personalities; I know damned well that the minute they get through with the analysis they'll get into the same trouble again. They don't take the time to shake out their body and hang it on the line, get a little air and sunlight into it.

I guess this is a philosophy of life I inherited from

my father. You must watch me play tennis before you leave, and go with me to the reservoir up in Beverly Hills. I think you honestly have to do that before you really know who or what I am.

You mentioned a story about Sinclair Lewis—

KATHARINE HEPBURN: Oh, yes. As I've implied, my parents were much more fascinating than I am, full of this and that. Dad would not serve liquor in the house during Prohibition; he was a stickler for certain rules. He would take a drink when someone else served it, however, so whether he was primarily an abstainer or a Scotsman was something I never figured out. But it caused a most incredible scene with Red Lewis.

Sinclair Lewis and his first wife moved into our neighborhood, and Mother was too busy with her marches or speeches or balloon-carrying or six children or whatever, to call on them. Finally they met at a party, and Red Lewis walked up to Ma and said, "Mrs. Hepburn, you and your husband are the two people here we've really wanted to meet, and you haven't come to call." Mother said, "Well, why don't you go home and I'll come to call on you." They went home, and Mother went. She came back about an hour later and told Dad that she had invited the Lewises to dinner Saturday night. He said, "Fine," and then Mother said, "We've got a terrible problem! Mr. Lewis drinks, you know, rather a great deal. What are we going to give him to drink? Can't we have some liquor —some whiskey?"

Dad went to the telephone, called Sinclair Lewis, and said, "I'm Dr. Hepburn, and I'm to be your host on Saturday night. I suggest that if you must get drunk to stand my company get drunk before you come because we don't serve liquor here." Mother was horrified. But the Lewises came—sober—and we saw a great deal of them after that.

I remember them well: I was twelve or thirteen and very shy and self-conscious, and Red Lewis was a very tall, thin man, awfully ugly, and he had a terrible complexion like an old turtle. Whenever he left the house I was expected to kiss his cheek, and it was all I could bring my lips to his face. I think he sensed my repugnance, and it must have hurt him terribly because he did so want to be loved. He was a darling lonely fellow.

All in all, I think I'm based upon an exquisitely happy childhood. All of us had it. Let Freud make what he wants to of *that*.

How many children were there?

KATHARINE HEPBURN: Six, altogether, but my older brother died at sixteen. So I'm the oldest, now, then my brother Dick, my brother Bob, my sister Marion (Kathy's mother), and my sister Peg.

How were you educated?

KATHARINE HEPBURN: The boys went to a country day school called Kingswood School. Private. I went to a public school, then to a girls' school called Oxford School, where Kathy also went.

When my brother died I left school and tutored for five years. That's how I got ahead and beyond where I'd have been otherwise. I would tutor in the morning and play golf with Dad in the afternoon. I became a very good golfer, but I didn't care too much for school. This made it difficult for me when I went to Bryn Mawr. I really wasn't used to people, and mingling was agony. I was very, very self-conscious. I roomed alone and was always a very early riser and very early to bed.

Dad said all my beaus were crashing bores; I would fall asleep about 7:30 in the evening, and he would have to entertain them, and he nearly died. I went to Bryn Mawr because Mother had gone there, but it was agony. It was excruciatingly painful to walk into the dining room to eat lunch; I'd nearly faint. (My father always said, "My children are very shy. They go to a party and are absolutely terrified that they are going to be neither the bride nor the corpse.) At school there is always a group of girls, at that age, who are sure of themselves, and they're apt to mistake what ails a kid who suffers as I did for arrogance. Perhaps the tone of my voice did it. I can remember walking into the Bryn Mawr dining room and hearing someone say, "Self-conscious beauty." I can even remember the outfit I wore; a french blue skirt buttoned down the front, and a blue and white Iceland sweater. My hair was the same as it is now—long, done up in a knob at the top. Now, I had never thought of myself as a beauty, though I certainly was self-conscious. The remark finished me. I spent all my allowance, after that, for eating out, and I never went into the dining room again. I couldn't even go into the john when anyone else was there. I got up very early to take my bath.

It was all very difficult. The only socializing I did came in my second year. I was part of a group called The Tenement, very much like The Group Mary McCarthy wrote about. (Her Group came about two years later at Vassar.) I always wondered about *The Group* because it was based so deeply in disillusionment. I didn't see that picture. I think that one does search for Aladdin and his lamp and for fairy tales; people are fundamentally romantic, and they may not achieve the romance, and may lose their sense of wonder. I was very fortunate. I was and am a romantic, and there've been times, naturally, when life hasn't lived up to expectations, but it's always a part that's let me down, never the whole. But again I credit my parents and that good childhood, and let Freud make what he wants of *that,* too.

If you suffered so terribly from shyness, how did you go into the theater?

KATHARINE HEPBURN: I don't know. Perhaps the two go together. I think many actors are very shy, but they have a strong urge either to express themselves or to hide behind the characters they play. Shyness is not uncommon in this profession; there are a lot of diffident people who act.

While I was at Bryn Mawr I went to a stock company which was run by Eddie Knopf, the brother of Alfred Knopf of the publishing firm. I had a letter of introduction; I gave it to him, and he said I should come back when I finished school.

Dad had always said, "Never write a letter if you want to get somewhere—go and appear." So I went, without even knowing there was a stage door to a theater. I went into the theater through the front door; they were having a rehearsal, and I sat there for four hours, in the middle, in back. I could see people escaping and entering all the time, but I didn't know how they were doing it. I thought I had the front of the building covered, that people had to come up or down one aisle or the other. Finally, Eddie Knopf came back and said, "What are you doing here?" I said, "I'm free, and you told me to come when I finished school." He said, "Okay, report for rehearsal on Monday."

I told Dad about the job I'd found in Baltimore, and he nearly had a stroke. He thought it was like taking to the streets. He thought it was a pretty feeble thing, that he'd hoped I'd amount to something. I'd saved up my allowances (all I hadn't spent on my furtive meals) and had just enough money to get by until they paid me something—two weeks, in that stock company. I played in a thing with Mary Boland, and after I'd been there a week Daddy sent me a letter with a check in it for $25. He said, "I won this gambling on the golf course, and I don't approve of gambling and I don't approve of what you're doing, so I think this money ought to be yours." (He was funny when I first said I wanted to go into the theater. He said, "Well, you've always liked to have people look at you. When we went off the first tee, if we were alone you might get a lousy shot, but if anyone was there to look at you, you'd take an extra look at the ball and clout it a mile.") In a way this is true of self-conscious people. One is affected by the presence of people. I know, for example, when there is a stranger on the set; I feel them immediately. Sometimes they annoy me, but if they look sort of sad I don't mind, and I never mention that they're around. But sometimes it just riles me to be stared at—or it embarrasses me. Especially when I'm doing a scene rather badly. I don't particularly approve of this characteristic; I find it very depleting.

If I can say more about this: I think one rebuilds himself when he is alone out in the wilderness. At least, I do. If I get any good ideas—if I'm writing anything, or figuring out a problem, or working on a script—those ideas come before I've spoken to anybody else in the morning. If I were a writer I would never speak to anyone in the morning; not until I'd finished working, say from 6:30 to noon. I find that the interference of conversation blunts the brain, just as the brain is affected if I read.

I never read notices. I never have read articles written about me because no matter how nice the writer is, he is bound to say something I can't put out of my mind. I played in a thing called *Death Takes a Holiday* in Philadelphia. I played the young girl (I was Kathy's age), and I was fired. My notices were evenly split. One said, "This lovely slim creature looking like Maude Adams came out on the stage last night and enchanted us." The other said, ". . . harsh voiced, skinny, unattractive girl . . . flounced across the stage and gave an idiotic performance." Philip Merivale, who starred in the play, said, "Don't read the notices. How are you going to react to them? Which one is right?" But the bad ones stick in your craw because you know that it's the person criticizing you who draws the most attention.

What happened after the play with Mary Boland?

KATHARINE HEPBURN: Next came some silly thing which had three idiotic flappers. I was rather bad in it, and I began to talk to people about how one goes about having a career. I thought my voice was very high—I would get excited, and it would shoot up into the top of my head. They suggested that I go to work in New York with a woman named Frances Robinson Duff. So I left the company after two weeks. (I'd gotten good notices in the Mary Boland play, *The Czarina*. The hell with what was said about me in the flapper business. Not important.) I wrote Dad and asked if he would be interested in backing such a project, and he said he would. He thought that if I was going to work in the theater it was some sign of intelligence to learn what the hell I was doing.

I went to New York and stayed with the widow of one of Dad's brothers and studied. Then Eddie Knopf closed the Baltimore stock company and moved to

New York to do a play, and they offered me a job as an understudy. I read the understudy part for them and they gave me the lead. This seemed perfectly logical to me; it was about time I became a star, since I'd been in the theater for over a week.

Imagine my ego! I rehearsed the role for two weeks. The play was wobbly, and that's how I got the role; they'd blamed the poor bloody leading lady for something she certainly wasn't to blame for, kicked her out, and put me in instead. The thing opened in Great Neck in a theater that all the theatrical producers used to go to on Saturday night. We were there for that one night.

I put on my face and did the first scene, including a rather long speech, after which the audience burst into applause. Quite right, I thought. But then I got excited, and began to deliver my lines faster and faster, and by the time I was into the second act nobody could understand a word I said. After the play I didn't think people appreciated me enough, and we went back to New York, and the next day I was fired.

After that I was hired by Arthur Hopkins, a remarkable man, for a small part in *These Days*. I got excellent reviews but the play only lasted three performances. I was still so dense that I thought because my notices were so good the play would have a long run; I didn't read the whole review, I guess, because I was so caught up with myself. I remember shrugging away the gloom everyone else felt, and standing, waiting for my entrance the second night, when an electrician came over and patted me on the shoulder and said, "Don't worry, dear, you'll be a big star someday." I thought, "What the hell is he talking about? I know I'm going to be a big star someday. Why is everyone so sad?" The closing notice had just gone up.

Arthur came to my rescue; he brought me to New Haven to understudy Hope Williams in *Holiday*. I remember Hope as an angel, a delightful and delicious person, and Philip Barry had written *Holiday* for her. And I understudied, still filled with a sense of my own importance.

You know, people make me laugh when they say that kids today have no respect for them. I had no respect for anyone, including John Barrymore. I think that sort of disrespect has always been there. It's a fundamental thing, because otherwise youngsters would be drowned by the older generation. They'd never amount to anything.

But I understudied Hope in *Holiday*—she offered to let me play the part, but I never did. I rehearsed it, once, in front of Arthur Hopkins, and he sat through it and said, "That was fine, dear. Never be sorry for yourself." This was his one criticism of what I had done. It was interesting criticism because a lot of kids are good emotional actors but achieve it by feeling sorry for themselves, and this is a very unattractive emotion. I'd thought I could do the emotional scenes better than Hope, so out went the stops.

After that a play with Jane Cowl; she even made me up to go onstage so that I'd look halfway decent, but it didn't work well enough to please the director, so they fired me. But a week later, when they couldn't find a suitable replacement, I was rehired and went on in New York. I played the ingenue; it was a richer part than the leading role Jane Cowl had, but she was an absolute angel to me. I got rave notices.

Jane taught me a great lesson. I've always had wonderful treatment from other actors. I think actors are incredibly generous. I have very, very seldom met an actor who would upstage me, or try to hurt me in another way. They try nothing but to make you better than you are. They're enormously kind, generous people.

From that I went to *The Animal Kingdom*—Philip Barry had written a part in it for me, but I got fired. Again. Leslie Howard took an instant dislike to me; I was very tall for an ingenue, and he didn't take kindly to this. I remember, at the first rehearsal, saying to him, "Mr. Howard, what would you like me to do then?" and he said, "My dear, I really don't give a damn." And I thought, "Oh, oh, this doesn't sound promising." And it wasn't. Then the Theater Guild let me understudy in *A Month in the Country,* Nazimova's beautiful production with Henry Travers and Dudley Diggs. I was with the Lunts in *Meteor,* at least I started out with them, but along came a part I thought would be more interesting in *Death Takes a Holiday* so I bowed out of *Meteor.* And promptly got fired from *Death Takes a Holiday.* Finally, that wonderful, magic thing, *The Warrior's Husband* and I was a star. At last.

How did you happen to go on to Hollywood?

KATHARINE HEPBURN: Rather early it was discovered that I photographed well. Once Paramount offered me a contract, but I turned them down because I had seen too many actors go to Hollywood to disappear. I decided that I would never go out there unless it was for a specific role I knew I could do. I was unconventional, certainly at the time very unconventional as compared to the actors in Hollywood, and I didn't really know what the hell they could put me in that wouldn't destroy me.

So I waited for the particular part, turning down tests and contract offers, but when I was playing in *The Warrior's Husband* David Selznick and George Cukor came along with an offer for the *Bill of Divorcement* test. They sent me the scene I was to play for the test, and I thought it an awful bore, and I thought, "Well, if they send this scene to every actress in New York they'll get bored looking at it over and over again." So I said, "No, I won't test in that scene. If you want me to test, let me pick my own material."

I called Alan Campbell—he wasn't yet married to Dorothy Parker—and said, "Alan, do a movie test with me. You'll sit in a wing chair and they won't even see you. You can read the part out of the book. I don't want you to get the part and me not to get the part. So they're just going to see me."

I went and was made up—covered with makeup, the way they did in those days. I did a scene from *Holiday,* which I knew backward. Then I decided that I looked idiotic in all that makeup, so I told them I would take their makeup off, put on my own to look more like myself, and do a silent test. I did. I still have this test I made in 1932 and it is absolutely heartbreaking. I look like someone in a state of total shock. Absurd. Desperate. First covered with makeup but determined to put on a good show. George Cukor said, later, that the only reason he ever hired me was because of the way I put down a glass.

I did that test, then a *Warrior's Husband* material test for Fox, which was absurd, and came out to play in *A Bill of Divorcement*. I signed to do another picture the following summer, if *Divorcement* proved successful, and at my own figure. I said I'd never go out there for less than $1,500 a week, and as it turned out I got it, and everything else I wanted. I was lucky. The part in *Bill of Divorcement* has made a star out of every woman who's played it. Kit Cornell did it, and Meggie Albanesi in London. It seemed calculated; Cornell, Albanesi, then me.

It really is rather fixed, in a way. Mine was an ingenue part; a star carried the play. And it's hard to carry something—it requires a great deal of stamina, and stamina doesn't show. But if you are new, if you haven't been seen before, and you have a wonderful part against the star, you practically always steal the play. Or the movie. There are lots of girls' parts written that way, so we naturally have a lot of girls who make a big hit in their first movie and lots of girls who've won the Academy Award their first year in the business. (Not so many boys; they're slower-starting, somehow, perhaps because they're not as attractive. A young girl is delicious, and a young boy is a bit of a bore. He comes along at twenty-eight, twenty-nine, thirty.)

My first year in Hollywood was a triumph. *A Bill of Divorcement, Morning Glory, Christopher Strong, Little Women*—all in a row. I won the Academy Award. It was a phenomenal year. And the next year was all right, and the year after that, plus the next two, but then came disaster, until Philip Barry came out to rescue me with *The Philadelphia Story*. You may remember when Marlene Dietrich and I were the chiefs of a group called "Poison at the Box Office." I was at RKO, and RKO was delighted to unload me, so they sent me a script they knew I would turn down, then made me pay them something to let me come over here to Columbia to do *Holiday*. I was very anxious to do *Holiday* with George Cukor. At this time I was getting $125,000 per picture and a percentage at RKO, but I bought my way out of my contract, made *Holiday* at Columbia, then went back home to Connecticut because I didn't have anything to do. While I was there MGM called and said they wanted me to do a picture for Lubitsch, and offered me $10,000. (Quite a drop in six short weeks.) I said, "Thank you very much. As a matter of fact, this is the first offer I've had, so you send along the script and I'll read it." I read it and wrote, "I'm sorry, but I just can't do it. It isn't the money. It's just that I really don't like the material, and since I failed on material that was dull, I can't do another bad film. I want to blame myself, now, for mistakes."

So I stayed playing golf at our summer place, Fenwick, at Saybrook, Connecticut. At the end of that year, 1938, the whole place was washed away in the hurricane. But before it had washed away, Philip Barry called and said he would like to see me. I thought, "What the hell does he want? This is queer." He said he had something to tell me. So we walked out to the end of the pier (we could never be alone in our house; too many people of all ages floating about). He said he had two plots. One was—God knows, I've forgotten. The other, *The Philadelphia Story*. I told him I liked *The Philadelphia Story,* and he asked me if I'd like to do it as a play. I said, "I might, if I don't do *Gone With the Wind.*"

George Cukor was going to direct *Gone With the Wind,* and David Selznick had sent for me and said, "We'd like you to do it, Kate." I said, "Now, David, I've had a lot of funny things happen to me, and I couldn't face signing a deal with you, now, and then three or four months from now have you pay me off because you've found the unknown girl. I'll tell you what I'll do: if you literally can't find anyone, and if you are two days from beginning the picture, I'll get Walter Plunkett to do the clothes for me and I'll be your Scarlett O'Hara." Of course, he found Vivien Leigh, and if I'd been signed for it he still would have found her, and he would have paid me off. And it would have been shattering. I would never have recovered my confidence.

No *Gone With the Wind,* but Philip sent me the first act of *The Philadelphia Story* and it was just great.

Then he sent me the second act and I didn't like it, so I called a pilot I used occasionally, and we flew up to the island off the Maine coast where Phil lived.

You know, it's very difficult to be honest with writers. Writers, after all, are writing the goddam stuff out of their imagination. It isn't even like criticizing an actor, because the actor is doing other people's material. But when you tell a writer you don't like what he's doing you are liable to throw him high, wide, and handsome. But since I was down so low and I had nothing whatever to lose, I said, "Well, Phil, I've read the second act and I think you've gone off on another play." I told him perfectly honestly and simply what I thought, and then I flew back home. A few days later he called me and said, "I agree with you," and in no time flat he sent me a new second act, in two scenes, and I thought it was great. We took it to New York, and I went to the Guild. (Phil didn't want to work with the Theatre Guild because he felt they had screwed up *Hotel Universe,* which was very close to his heart. But I felt that I had to take it to them because they had been willing to close *Jane Eyre* out of town because I didn't want to come in in it. Phil went along.)

(During my first movie career I returned to the stage with *The Lake,* a total disaster, and some sort of puritan force drove me back—the theater has always terrified me—to do *Jane Eyre*. It wasn't right. Because I was a star it drew capacity audiences, but it didn't jell, and I did not want to go to New York with it. But Brooks Atkinson, immoral fellow, came to Chicago to review it, which he shouldn't have done because we were closing it out of town. So I didn't miss getting roasted in New York, anyway, thanks to Brooks.)

The Guild took *The Philadelphia Story* and began to cast it, and Phil went to Florida to write the third act. We had everybody in it: Shirley Booth, Joseph Cotten,

Van Heflin, Anne Baxter (who was replaced later because we needed a kid about nine years old, and Anne was sixteen or seventeen). One night Phil called me—we weren't pressuring him—and asked how things were going. I said, "Very, very slowly, Phil. We haven't gotten anywhere, much. We've read some interesting people, but we haven't got much of anywhere." Actually, we had the cast. But some good angel spoke to me to handle Phil that way. Later he told me he was hung up. He could think of nothing. "They're casting, they're waiting for me," and he was blanked. Being let off the hook a little released the pressure, and he sat down and wrote that beautiful third act. I learned a lot about handling people from that.

But at any rate, *The Philadelphia Story* was a smash on the stage and very successful as a film, and I don't think I've been box office poison since then. Of course, I haven't made too many pictures. A total of twenty-seven in thirty-five years. I haven't overexposed myself.

> *The public has associated you with three actors during your career—Cary Grant, as a result of* Holiday; *Humphrey Bogart, in* The African Queen; *and Spencer Tracy, through the nine films you've made with him. Could you describe these men in your own terms?*

KATHARINE HEPBURN: Well, Spencer Tracy just *is*. He is the most remarkable actor ever born. He is one of the few people capable of total concentration. It's all based on the truth. It's all as simple as "thank you" in the full meaning of the word. He's the same in the theater and in movies. The two are really very similar, I think; there isn't this vast difference in technique you hear about. Spencer and Laurette Taylor are my idea of the two best actors I've ever seen, given any country you'd care to mention. You are simply present at something. It's a happening. It has nothing to do with apparent planning, yet it is the result of total concentration. Spencer will read the script over and over and over again, but he doesn't decide, as some actors do, "I'm going to lift my hand and scratch my nose at this point." In the first place he wouldn't understand how you would know that you were going to reach up to scratch your nose, until you found out what the other fellow was going to do in the scene.

Bogey was a very interesting actor. He was one of the few men—and I'm spelling "men" with a capital M—I've ever known who was proud of being an actor. (I think it has upset Spencer that he's been an actor.) Bogey thought it was great, that it was a fine profession. And Bogey was quite right. Spencer has been wrong.

Bogey was totally concentrated as an actor, but he was acting. He didn't have the incredible concentration of Spencer. They were of different castes. Spencer is in a state of concentration so deep that it comes out totally simple. Bogey's work was based, a little, on Bogey's personality. I don't mean in a cute or affected way. It was an actor functioning, and Spencer is the man functioning—both in the best sense of the word, taking nothing away from either. But there was this difference.

Cary Grant, I think, is a personality functioning. A delicious personality who has learned to do certain things marvelously well. He can't play a serious part or, let me say, the public isn't interested in him that way, not interested in him at all, which I'm sure has been a big bugaboo to him. But he has a lovely sense of timing and an amusing face and a lovely voice. He discovered that personality in *Sylvia Scarlett,* with George Cukor, who cast him in it, cast him as the man he was, a cockney sort of guy. (It's an interesting film, but a total disaster; it's never made back a nickel. I played a boy all the way through.) But it made a star of Cary. George Cukor says, when people say, "You know, I like *Sylvia Scarlett,* that gives me a line on you. You're one of The Group."

As far as relations with the press are concerned, you and Garbo have been, consistently, rather elusive. Is this due to the shyness you mentioned, or have you actively disliked the press?

KATHARINE HEPBURN: When I first came to Hollywood I thought the press was asinine. The studio wanted me to give a lot of interviews, but the press didn't know who the hell I was, thank God, so they couldn't track me down, and I didn't see anybody. Actually, I wanted to see whether I was going to be successful or not before I gave a lot of interviews.

After I finished *A Bill of Divorcement* I went to Europe, and when I was in Vienna they sent me a wire, telling me I was a big hit. I was traveling steerage; I never traveled first class because I always got seasick, and to throw up on first class fare seemed rather silly. But I thought it would really look peculiar if I came back to the U.S. in my rags, tumbling out of steerage, so I got a first-class ticket and came back looking very kosher.

The press met me and asked, I thought, idiotic questions. So I gave them idiotic answers. And they asked me things that I didn't think were any of their damned business, so I'd make up some ludicrous answer which I thought they'd be bright enough to see through. But they didn't. They just printed everything.

I felt, then, that the press was my natural enemy. This may have been because of the notices I got in the first things I did, the things I kept getting fired from. I don't know. I really don't know because Mother, God knows, with all the causes she fought for, constantly struggled to get the press on her side, struggled to get mentioned. Yet I've always had this terrible antipathy toward the press.

I had a great sense of privacy. I didn't think they had any business to know certain things, and the things they wanted to know about movie actors in those days (and the things they still want to know) amounted to titillating bits of gossip. And I didn't think the corners of my private life belonged to them.

But I'm afraid we really have no way of obtaining privacy because the public wants to read such awful things. Both *Valley of the Dolls* and Kazan's *The Arrangement* are just straight pornography. Polite pornography. No merit of any kind in either book, from my point of view. They are rottenly written. It disgusts me that somebody with Kazan's potential should stoop to becoming such a mutt; disgusting because he is an enormously talented man. For him to write that kind of balderdash is sickening; I think it must be deeply disillusioning to the entire human race. And I always felt that Kazan was rather interested in the human race. I just don't think that men of brains and position have the right to turn out a book like that. But that stuff sells. All that stuff about Dickie and Liz sells. What did I start to say? I'm off the track.

In my heyday, you know, when they were chasing me around and I traveled with some other flamboyant characters, that same sort of stuff sold. But they never caught me. They never got on my trail. They were even in the wrong cities and in the wrong states and on the wrong streets, because I would go to a great deal of trouble to keep out of their way. It wasn't just a game with me, because it made me goddam sore.

When I discovered that the studio gave out the information as to my whereabouts even the studio lost any source of information, and they never knew whether I was coming or going. And I traveled by automobile a great deal. When I took a train I always got off before the train came into the main station. You can outwit the press, you know. A lot of this stuff about people claiming to be tortured by the press is silly; they've asked for it. I've traveled all over the world and had wonderful times, and the press never caught me.

Perhaps this insistence upon privacy has helped maintain an image for both you and Garbo, and created the legends.

KATHARINE HEPBURN: I don't think I am or can be a legend or an image in the same manner as Garbo. I think I've been around long enough and worked hard enough, and I suppose people may be rather fond of me as they are of an old building.

But Garbo is the total mystery. She is, to me, the way actors should be. I don't think actors should ever be seen, and she went out of her way not to be seen, more or less the way I did.

But I did not want my life to be dominated totally by my career. I did not want to change my way of living because of my career, and I think I resented the press so much because they pried into my personal life. Garbo has gone to even more trouble to keep the press away, but this is not only because of her personality but because of the parts she's played—the mysterious creature. The illusion, the aloofness, is needed.

I'm a legend simply because I've survived over a long period of time and still seem to be the master of my fate. I'm still paddling the goddamned boat myself, you know; I'm not sitting being paddled by anyone. It may only be a canoe, but nevertheless, I'm paddling it, whereas Garbo has always been a mysterious sailboat who disappeared over the horizon the moment she felt she couldn't cope. She represented a kind of elusive beauty, and she felt, I think, that when that elusive beauty started to fade she should wave good-bye and disappear. Or maybe she simply didn't want to do anything else.

I can understand that. But I wouldn't put myself in the class with Garbo. I think I'm okay, but not as the mysterious figure of the late twenties, thirties, and early forties. There were very few of those magic figures, you know. But they had to be foreign. That had to be part of the mystery. I'm American, after all. This is my country. I have as much right to walk around in it as anyone else, and I would always feel that. Hell, I'm at home, and all of a sudden they may have put me up on a pedestal, but it didn't mean I had to stay on the pedestal. I hopped down—hopefully into my private life.

If I went to the theater, for example, I would never give autographs. I did not want to cause a lot of confusion around me, and I didn't think anyone at the theater had a right to ask for an autograph. Finally they got accustomed to that fact. I'd say, "Shut up. No, I'm not going to give it to you," or "Go and sit down. You make me feel like an ass."

Perhaps I've been such a nut on the subject of privacy because I know you can get terribly spoiled in this business, and what are you going to do when it all ends? You're sort of a Golden Girl for awhile, but you can't stay the Golden Girl for five-hundred years, and if you've taken the Golden Girl business too seriously you can be terribly thrown. Yet when I was the Golden Girl I still wanted to be able to go through that damned Art Institute in Chicago (and I bloody well did, every time I went through Chicago). I'd walk through it and when people approached I'd say, "Don't you bother me. I have as much right to be here as you have. Leave me alone." Otherwise I'd have to go. "What do you want to do? Chase me out?" And they'd leave me alone. And that was honest, wasn't it? Now, if I was off on a romantic voyage and the press caught a glimpse of me with some tall, dark stranger, and saw the luggage—well, I took great care that they never did. I've never gone to public places to eat because I can eat at home. But I could never go to the theater or to the Art Institute at home.

Fortunately, I loathe eating out, otherwise I'd have caused disturbances in restaurants, too. I've eaten out about six times and I've passed out at least half those times. Fainted dead away. Ridiculous. I know it hasn't been the snails, because I've survived. Just nerves. Perhaps eating at home suits me best because I'm a terribly heavy eater.

But I've never wanted to be the Golden Girl, off the screen. I've never dressed up, off the screen. I've always bought my own tickets and lived in a way I could afford to live.

I think Garbo has done this, too. But as a legend she's in a class by herself.

In a similar way, speaking of images and legends, the public firmly associates you and Spencer Tracy as a sort of perfect team. Your long friendship is acknowledged, but I think all the pictures you've made together have established an "ideal relationship" concept.

KATHARINE HEPBURN: I think we represent the perfect American couple. Certainly the ideal American man is Spencer. Sports-loving, a man's man. Strong looking, a big sort of head, boar neck, and so forth. A man. And I think I represent a woman. I needle him, and I irritate him, and I try to get around him, yet if he put a big paw out he could squash me. I think this is the sort of romantic, ideal picture of the male and female in the United States. I'm always sort of skitting about, and he's the big bear, and every once in awhile he turns and growls and I tremble. And every once in a while he turns and says some terrible thing and everybody laughs at me, and I get furious. It's very male-female; I think that must be it. And on that basis it's very solid; people can see themselves in us. Married couples can see themselves in us. The woman always wanting to be—oh, the great columnist, the great sportswoman, the great lawyer. Competing and yet not competing. Certainly most of the pictures Garson Kanin and Ruth Gordon wrote for us were like that. The woman very quick, on to everything, ready to go forward with anything, emotional. The man slower, more solid, very funny at times, good with quips, ultimately subduing the woman, thereby making her happy because she really wanted to be subdued, or at least to let him think she's being subdued.

Do you find a difference between the personalities, the stars, that came up during your earlier eras in films, and those that are coming on now?

KATHARINE HEPBURN: I don't think there's a hell of a lot of difference. I think that styles and personalities change. Both Marlene and I wore pants, and she wore a tuxedo and silk hat to a nightclub. I adored that, and I'm amused by Julie Christie appearing at the Academy Awards in a short skirt with her hair all over her eyes. It's kind of fun, you know. And it's for the same reason. Marlene is a wonderful show creature. Unique. She has her own personality. Pants and short skirts get noticed. Noticed and remembered.

As far as I went, however, I could never stand wearing dresses, and I don't like stockings; I can't keep them up. That's the thing that first started me going around wearing pants. And I don't like high heels, either. I like great big boots, like these I'm wearing now.

If I went to the theater in the evening I would wear a dress. But a matinee—pants. I tried not to be too conspicuous.

You know, it's kind of the style to be a nut, now, and I've always rather liked nuts. I was a nut in my day, just by wearing pants, though it didn't seem nutty to me. It seemed sensible. And now, when I think of a little face with hair tumbling all over it and eyes peeking out of it—that's rather fun. However, I'd sooner have a skirt tumble all over ugly, short legs, so that I peek at the feet, than have those sturdy, dumpy legs hit me in the face. If a woman has Marlene's legs, show them. But there are many legs we are forced to look at, today, that would be better left unseen. And let's face it—a knee is a knee is a knee is a joint—cover it up.

I do think that people have gotten awfully unfussy about what they display. It used to be the style, in my day, for people with bosoms smaller than mine to take their blouses off on the screen. (I have a rather small bosom and I wasn't about to display it.) Nobody ever asked me to take my shirt off to take a peek at me and that was fine. Now, you'll notice that Sophia and Marilyn don't take their shirts off on the screen. Never. That, you see, would really be an erotic experience. But if those girls with those little bosoms take their shirts off it's just kind of sad, as though they can't get anybody to look at them unless they do.

It's a funny situation, isn't it? Only the tremendously undersexed do things like that. It's a tremendous lack of sexuality.

So much talk about sex. The four-letter words we've all become inured to, by now. All this desperate effort to be titillating. I don't know what is intended, but it's exhausting because it just means one thing to me: impotence. You know, the man that can do it doesn't talk about it, and that happens to be the truth. It's a sad comment, very sad. Because I think however far they go, whatever they photograph, whatever they write, they are not going to be able to explain the magics of life. And the magics of life are the things that dominate us—birth, love, death, and self-sacrifice. Those are the beautiful things we can't even describe, the things that dominate our lives, the things that, in the long run, make the wheels of the world go around. Call it religion. (The religious people try to explain it all in terms of God.) I try to do it on the basis of man. I believe in the goodness of man, the infinite goodness of man. I don't think it varies much from generation to generation. I think customs vary a lot. They say, now, that the sexual behavior of the young has become dangerous. My observations have been that the degree of difference from one generation to another is relatively slight. My mother always said that the only things she regretted were the things she hadn't done. And I'm with her there.

I guess I've known many women who were supposed to be wicked, who were darling creatures, generous, sweet, nice people. And I've known women who'd led too-virtuous lives who have been nowhere near as charming. You know, there comes an age when you begin to look around at the world, not just at yourself—twenty-eight, thirty-five, it varies with individuals—and I hate to see people reach that point doing things which I know are going to give them terrible complexes, but at the same time I hate to see them inhibited, not living.

What are the most notable changes that have taken place in the motion picture world since you came out here?

KATHARINE HEPBURN: So many. In the old days you could carry a bad picture, if you were a star, to the point where the company at least got its money out. Now if a picture is bad enough people will not go. It doesn't make any difference who is in it, with the possible exception of Elizabeth Taylor.

There aren't many real stars now, in movies or in theater. Elizabeth is; she can draw in something that isn't very good. There are lots of talented people, but few whom I would call real, total stars. Today a conglomeration of good people is more important than the name of an actor.

At first, when I went to RKO, that studio was in a very uncertain state. It had six presidents in five years, a matter of constant change, but they used to do very interesting pictures. Little pictures. *Alice Adams* cost $350,000; *A Bill of Divorcement* about $400,000 because of Jack Barrymore's salary; *Little Women* $495,000. (A big picture—great sets. It wasn't in color because they didn't have color then, but it certainly was everything a picture could be.) *Morning Glory* cost $217,000 and was made in seventeen days and we never worked beyond 5:30 in the afternoon.

At Metro I was brought up in a sort of paternalistic system. Very posh. They were producing excellent pictures; for the stars it was like being at a wonderful boarding school, never graduating, just being kept mildly occupied. Think of the stars they had then—

Garbo, Shearer, Crawford, Harlow, Dressler, Beery, Gable, Tracy. Incredible.

Now, of course, the big studio, the paternalistic set-up, is gone. And it's petrifying the way the production of pictures in this country has become so goddam expensive. The films have to make back so much money. A *Mary Poppins* costs a lot but makes it back, and it's great, but it would terrify me if I were spending nine or ten million dollars of someone else's money. I think it's too bad they have to cost that much. I think we'd be further ahead if we could make more modestly priced pictures with the same people. I don't think Richard and Elizabeth got paid all that when they did *Taming of the Shrew*. Sure, they owned a chunk of it, but that isn't the same thing. That's healthy. The cost of the picture wasn't astronomical, and I think other actors should follow that route.

Because of costs I'm afraid we're avoiding making films that are either fillers or innovators. I hate to see the European market produce all the things like *Shop on Main Street, Georgy Girl,* and *Alfie*. I think it's too bad that we can't, in this country, compete with that market and produce a picture that doesn't have to appeal to so many people. Because if you're selling an article that has to be bought by a great many people, you can't make it in an odd shape because not many people will like an odd shape. They won't buy it. So we have to hold down our imagination a great deal, and it's quite difficult. And the exceptions prove the rule; *Lilies of the Field* cost very little money, yet it did quite well.

I think there are times when all of us should take a cut, and times when we should be paid a great deal. For instance, when I played *As You Like It* I cut my salary and said, "Pay me what you can afford to pay me," because I didn't know what kind of business it would draw. That was my contract with the Theatre Guild.

Do you share what seems to be a popular conception that men like Louis B. Mayer and Harry Cohn were tyrants?

KATHARINE HEPBURN: No. I don't. They made good pictures and they knew what they were doing and they were stagestruck. They certainly knew more than the actors, and some of the time their judgments were sound. I don't mean that they weren't sometimes cruel, or that they were incapable of bad judgments. But they usually knew more than the men in New York who tried to control them and the people they employed who they had to control. But in this business—I like tyrants—they start things, I might add, and get finished by them. All but Sam Goldwyn, he's the most remarkable of all of them. He backed his own judgment with his own money.

How did the film Guess Who's Coming to Dinner *come to you, and what made you decide to do it? What are your own feelings concerning the theme?*

KATHARINE HEPBURN: Stanley Kramer came to Spencer and me at the same time to talk about the film, which at that time was an original concept by William Rose. He asked us if we would be interested in the film, told us there was a possibility he could get Sidney Poitier. We said yes, we were interested, particularly after he told us the plot, with which we agreed in principle.

I must say that I haven't known any colored person particularly well. I've never had one as a friend. But I can't see any difference and I'm sure there isn't any difference. It's all a question of a man is a man is a man. I have to believe the speech I have in the picture where I say there is no essential difference betwen blacks and whites and yellows and reds. I think it's, at best, an economic state and a matter of mental development. I know Sidney, and I can't consider Sidney as a Negro—he's just Sidney. He's not black, he's not white, he's nothing at all as far as color is concerned.

The concept of the picture appeals to me because I think the only solution to the integration problem is intermarriage and disappearance. For example, there has been a lot of intermarriage between Christians and Jews in the past thirty to forty years. It was considered a bit odd and disappointing to the Jews, odd and disappointing to the Christians. But nobody thinks anything of it anymore. They used to say, "Unfortunately, he's Jewish." Now they say, "Unfortunately, he's colored." And I think this will cease to be.

In my childhood they said, "Unfortunately, he's Catholic." I can remember having a Catholic beau, and my father nearly died because the Catholics have a tradition of being rather reactionary, as you know. They are always on the slower side. Mind you, not about the colored people—they have an open door. I think they have a colored cardinal. That's why they decided to have a monsignor in the picture. The Catholics have been open in their policy toward colored people, but in the old days, when I was young, my family regarded the Catholics as taboo because they were against everything. They were against birth control, against the vote for women, always on the side of the diehards. While the Jews, of course, especially the rabbis, were always in the forefront as far as reform went. My family, remember, was and is a family of reformers. I was extremely conscious of anything that worked against reform, which the Catholics did during my childhood.

As transportation becomes so much faster and easier and cheaper we're bound to settle for the true worth of persons and discover that every personality is different. The bigoted white person will try to claim that Negroes are stupid, lazy, not above stealing, and without responsibility. But there are all too many white people who are stupid, lazy, not above stealing, and without responsibility. I don't think these are the characteristics of the Negro race at all.

I made a picture in Africa, and I know there is one characteristic the Negroes have which is wonderful and basic: the desire and ability to make people feel wonderfully about themselves. They have a very warm and appreciative point of view. I think that when the bulk of them get out of the rut they've been kept in they're going to snag all the public relations jobs because they're brilliant about remembering people. When you drive into New York, across one of the bridges, there's a colored policeman at the gate who says, "Miss Hepburn, you're back. How nice." They know I drive up to Connecticut every weekend when I'm there and all the Negroes I meet make me feel at home. This quality is straight out of the jungle; they had it in the jungle when I made *The African Queen*. A little man named Taihli Bacomba took care of me, and we conversed in very bad French, but he had this same strong personal regard. A lovely quality.

I think a film like *Guess Who's Coming to Dinner* constitutes a step in the right direction. It places the situation right on the table. It really attacks petty snobbery. In the picture, you know, Spencer is opposed to the marriage. I think this is characteristic, because men are much more cautious than women. And I think it is very interesting that the colored wife and the white wife have the same attitude. They sort of say, "We'll take a chance, let's see what happens. They are in love, and that is the most important thing of all." Spencer, again in the picture, is against it, not on a snobbish basis but because he thinks, "My God, the problems they're going to face!" But then he decides to let them face the problems because the problems have to be ameliorated. We are going to have to amalgamate.

Heavens, a great many whites and blacks are intermingled already. I have always felt sorry that the colored people can have freckles, too. I used to feel that to be white and spotted was dreadful, but to be colored and spotted must be just as bad. So I'm afraid that intermarriage isn't about to solve the freckle problem.

Who are the people in your life who have been helpful, influential, or even inspirational?

KATHARINE HEPBURN: There are so many—from so many aspects. Professionally, a teacher named Alfred Dixon, and Constance Collier. I worked with Constance on all the Shakespearean things I did. She and I had met several times at George Cukor's, and once Lawrence Langner talked to me and said, "You know, Kate, if you don't do something that matters in the big world of the theater it's going to pass you by and you'll regret that you never did it. I think you should play *As You Like It.*" So I decided to stick my neck out, and I went to George and said, "I wonder if Constance would work with me." George asked her, she agreed, and we started working together.

It was enormously rewarding. And thrilling. She was a fund of information and a very sympathetic human being. She was a remarkable character, with real nerve. Her eye was so high off the ground it carried a body that was ill and legs that shouldn't have moved. Dad used to say, "She bounces on those stumps through sheer character. She can't have any feeling in them." Even when she was blind as a bat she kept going. She had no feeling in her fingers. Once she picked up a butter ball instead of a roll. She tasted it and thought, "Good God I've picked up a butter ball." But she ate it, pretending to a neighbor who was watching her that she actually *wanted* to eat the butter ball.

Constance could never say no. You'd call her up and ask her to a preview, and she'd say, "Oh, yes, I'll get dressed. It's only 2:00 A.M. What's the difference." She was a very affirmative person.

(I'm rather cautious, oddly enough. I say No, no, no. But once I say yes the person is automatically a familiar. But my first impulse is to say no.)

The rewards of Shakespeare (if I may digress) which Constance and Lawrence Langner led me to, were enormous. Thrilling experiences. I think it's a pity that they haven't got a real classical theater here, but I think we will have. I think it's unfortunate that plays cost so much to do. But we're gradually developing an audience for the classical, so we'll have a national theater to meet its needs. It takes a bit of doing; it isn't easy to come by.

We've rather sneered at classical training in this country, with the result that there are a lot of actors who can't speak well enough to do the classics. Cultivated people who should be able to speak well enough can't do it.

When my mother was young at Bryn Mawr, and when I was a kid, people worked on their speech. They had a professor named Samuel Arthur King. He had a course in reading aloud; everyone had to take it.

This is where I developed my speech pattern beside

being a New Englander, I suppose. Tallulah Bankhead once told me that when she went into a theater where I was appearing she wondered, "Why the hell does Katie talk that way?" and when she came out she'd wonder, "Why the hell doesn't *everyone* talk that way?"

It became the style, you know, to be the common man—for everyone to belong to a labor union or to talk like a gangster. Proper speaking went out. I think this was too bad because the people who do have a proper voice automatically have a great deal going for them. Think of Kennedy's voice. It was charming, and his enunciation was correct and rather highbrow. Harvard. And people liked it. People liked FDR; the voice had breeding and confidence and it inspired confidence.

Johnson's voice is very much against him—his delivery and colloquialisms—too much Texas. I think Wendell Willkie flopped because of his voice. And think of how people, Americans included, adored listening to Churchill.

Even on a mass-audience program, like Ed Sullivan's, a voice will steal the show. When he has a really marvelous opera star—that star gets the biggest applause. People respond to a voice, love a voice; a voice inspires confidence. I think we, in this country, should use our voices to speak properly and pleasantly. It's unfortunate, the ideal of the mutt. Thinking everybody is as good as everybody else. Very bad.

I remember my sister saying, once, to me, "You know, your rather prissy voice makes people think you're a snob." I don't think they do, at all. I think people respect certain qualities and like to better themselves. Your working class is working like hell to better itself. They want to decorate their houses and be the queen in the castle. I think we should set our standards high, not lower them. Otherwise, you're dead. You can never be good enough. (None of us in this picture can ever be really as good as Bill Rose imagined when he wrote it.) You can't stay with the common man, and I think this is why the Democratic Party has drawn so far ahead. It's aimed higher for the common man. The Republicans have usually aimed for the status quo, and the status quo is a bore. You can't stand still.

End of digression.

People who have helped—so many. George Cukor, as both a friend and a director of so many of the films I've been in, has been magnificent. He is a truly beautiful person. Inside. He would never harm anyone; he has consideration and gentleness that is the mark of real humanity, and he has a real love for this business and a gift for it.

People who have been inspirational—I don't know who would have had a definite effect upon me, but I think that Jesus Christ and Queen Elizabeth are the two people I've admired most. Christ I admire enormously because I admire the principle of living for other people. It brings such definite results; I think it's the real answer instead of the Freudian business. I think the less we delve into ourselves the happier we're going to be. Which is an odd thing to say, being in this business where we're apt to be so preoccupied with ourselves.

Queen Elizabeth fascinates me—how she survived in the situation into which she was born; her capacity to wait, even as a kid, before she made up her mind, before she acted. She was never in too much of a hurry to make a judgment, a decision. I've rather followed that philosophy. I've never artificially made up my mind to do something that I haven't lived to regret. I've got to have something push me, something that says, "This is the thing to do, you've got to do it."

A conviction that comes from somewhere. Arbitrary decisions I've always regretted.

Now, obviously, if you ask me who has influenced me most, I'd have to say—and you know this from all I've told you—my mother and father. I'm the complete result of a father and mother who were wonderful people, the result of a completely happy childhood. I'm the best ad in the world for that sort of upbringing, because it influences me in practically every move I make, and not in a sloppy way, but in a wonderful way. You see, I admired them very much as people as well as loving them very much as parents. They were real friends.

Katharine Hepburn's home is in New York and Connecticut. In California she has the Birdcage which is, in reality, a birdcage built by John Barrymore. (A leaded stained-glass window still glows, rather sadly, with a "portrait" of Barrymore and Dolores Costello.) The house is part of the Barrymore estate, high up in Beverly Hills, screened from the curious by a tall, gated metal fence and a thick growth of shrubbery. One climbs up to the entry past an assortment of tubs, pots, and the (oddly decorative) inside of an old washing machine, all planted with roses, sweet peas, and a variety of other blooms, carefully nurtured by Katharine.

The enormous living room, once the Barrymore aviary, she uses for painting. Perfectly proportioned, parqueted with mellow, aged wood, and high ceilinged, it is generously illuminated by a series of skylights.

About twenty of her paintings are displayed here and in an adjoining room. Depending upon the subject (portrait, still life, or landscape) and the mood, her extremely well-executed oils bring fleeting reminders of Manet, Monet, Sisley, and Renoir. Perspectives are good, colors rich, approaches traditional. Especially effective are two portraits of her secretary, Phyllis Wilborn (once Constance Collier's secretary and a fascinating woman in her own right).

Katharine made tall glasses of iced tea and we talked again.

KATHARINE HEPBURN: As I mentioned, I'm always amused when I hear people talk about how disrespectful young people are, as though a lack of veneration for adults was born yesterday. I think youngsters have always shown a basic lack of respect, and I think it's necessary. If they didn't they wouldn't grow; they'd just repeat patterns, and the patterns any adult generation has developed are far from perfect.

I remember—especially sitting here in this room—how I felt about John Barrymore when I came to Hollywood as a very callow girl. I was Kathy's age, and when we started filming a scene he played it rather badly, I thought—hammy. Well, you're not much good! That's phony. As coldly as that. Here he was, the great Jack Barrymore, being sweet to me, and I thought, "Well, you're overrated."

The scene that caused this was when he'd escaped from the lunatic asylum and came to the house, and he was fishing about on the mantlepiece trying to find his pipe. I came into the room through a little door; I'd never seen him, as a grown-up girl, and he turned around and looked at me for a long time and said, "Do you know who I am?" and I said, "I think you're my father." It's a shattering line, if you really think about it. They were on Jack, and I was off-camera with tears pouring down my face. Jack was very exaggerated. He looked at me, walked over to me, and took my face in his hand, and said to George Cukor, "I'd like to do it again." I thought, "Well, you're just a big hambone. You're phony. But I guess they must have liked this sort of thing in your day." Then he went back and did it again, and it was absolutely shattering, and all of my disrespect melted away. But I think, as a youngster, you have to doubt all the values and dispute all the standards before you accept anything at all. God knows the adult generations of today haven't exactly created a world that kids should step into, no questions asked. They have a right to ask lots of questions.

Getting back to Jack, I think life was an awful burden to him. He was enormously talented, but he couldn't really center on anything. He'd center on *Hamlet,* do it brilliantly, but the day after it opened he was no longer interested in it. Arthur Hopkins, who was a great friend of mine, and did *Hamlet* and *Richard III* with Jack, and knew him very well, said that nothing was too much trouble for him. He'd go, on his lunch hour, to try on a sword and have it fitted and set at the proper angle and make sure his boots were perfect, everything in absolute order, but the day after the opening he was an absolute nervous wreck and finished with the play. He had great satisfaction at having pulled it off, but no enduring satisfaction. He was a tortured, talented man.

One day, on the set, you remarked that you haven't felt "like an actress" as far as professional dedication is concerned. How did you mean that?

KATHARINE HEPBURN: I think it's a very fortunate part of my nature that I've been that way. Dedicated, but not sublimated. Whatever I do at the moment is it. Wholehearted. With absolute concentration. Maybe it's the training, the Scotch-English-Welsh heritage. I don't know.

I do know that when I see someone dance divinely, that I'd like to be a dancer and forget all about acting. (It's a bit too late for that, now.)

Whatever I'm doing I like enormously. I don't yearn for something I haven't got. I'm always fascinated by doing something new. Waxing this floor gives me an enormous amount of satisfaction. I don't feel that I have to be the greatest actress in the world or the greatest whatever; I get just as much fun out of growing flowers in those goddam barrels outside. Flowers in a place where there shouldn't be a garden. When you have to put down, on one form or another, your profession, I always feel like putting down whatever I'm doing at the moment.

I took up painting in 1936 or 1937. I was in a situation which I thought would be extremely dull, and I was right. I bought myself a box of paints, thinking, "I must protect myself somehow." Otherwise I knew I'd have gone mad.

I could probably, I hope—or do I kid myself?—be a good painter if I had the time. It totally absorbs me when I do it. More than anything in the world.

We have an odd way of talking and thinking, now, in this country. The workweek has gotten shorter, the workday shorter, and more and more people say, "I just don't know what to do with myself." All this leisure, and they don't have sense enough to fill it with anything but boredom. It's terrifying. And their aches and pains. "I don't know what's the matter with my stomach" or it's their feet or their head or their you-know-what. (The twenty-four-year-old boy with prostate trouble is *really* astonishing; that sort of thing shouldn't come up until he's sixty.) What's wrong with them isn't in their body; it's in their head.

What the hell are people going to do with all their idle time unless they develop a philosophy of living? And a capacity to enjoy life? Medicare at thirty-five, just because they haven't got sense enough to keep their body in tune?

Even more frightening is the way they build these isolated Alcatrazes for the old and inveigle those poor people out to a place where they can't have a dog or hear a child. They sit and stagnate in total comfort. Total comfort is not what anybody wants; we want contrast.

It's going to be very fascinating to see what people do in this insurance company concept of retirement. We have so many people who are very good at their professions or crafts, who are on one track. They almost have to be on one track, put total attention to one thing, to get anywhere in this country because between the specialization and the competition and the knowledge explosion a twenty-four-hour day isn't enough.

I think insurance companies have spelled the end to decency in America. Take those absurd tables and statistics that add up to enforced retirement at the age of sixty-five. Some men are ready for retirement at forty-five, some at fifty-five, some never. The professional man, the truly skilled and dedicated man, is often at the peak of his power at sixty-five, and think of the terrible waste that comes about by taking him away from his job. I think it would be kinder to line him up against a wall and shoot him than thrust him into enforced idleness. For my part, I won't go to a doctor who's under fifty; I think it takes that long for a physican to really know what it's all about, and I don't care to feel like an experiment for some youngster.

Also part of the insurance company morality—take these asinine damage and liability claims. When you visit my house I would expect you to be responsible for your own physical conduct. If you slip and fall it should be accepted as a matter of your carelessness, not my responsibility. Yet the insurance all of us have to carry, just in case someone injures himself on our property. It's disgraceful!

But to get back to the point—no, except when I'm acting, I don't regard myself as an actress. When I'm washing the ceiling I'm totally preoccupied with being a ceiling-washer. And you must watch me play tennis, because when I play I think it is the most thrilling thing in the world, and I'm at it 100 percent. Perhaps the way I play tennis is the real key to my character.

Yet you're totally absorbed in Guess Who's Coming to Dinner.

KATHARINE HEPBURN*:* It's in character, I think. Although there's a lot to do. I'm trying to think for Kathy, too. To watch and see that she doesn't muck up anything just through not knowing about it, a thing I might catch, just through experience.

I also feel an obligation to Stanley; if, in reading the script over and over again I find anything I think is a contribution to the picture as a whole, wonderful; the whole interests me more than any individual part of it. When you start out you think of nothing but your own part; you have no idea that anything else exists. Gradually you realize that no matter how good your part is, no matter how good you are, if the entire vehicle isn't solid beneath you it's not going to last.

I'm still often struck by the resemblance between you and your niece, Katharine Houghton. It's like having a twenty-two-year-old Hepburn back on the scene.

KATHARINE HEPBURN: My mouth is bigger, but the tooth line is the same, and the general placement of the features, and the way the nose springs out of the face and her eyes are beautiful and mine are just eyes. Kathy complains about her voice; says, "Everybody thinks you have a beautiful voice and I have no voice at all," and I've told her, "When I was your age everybody said, 'Isn't it a shame Kate's voice isn't like her mother's.' You'll catch up."

Voice is part of the actor's agony. I've told Kathy that she should really study Shakespeare. When I got the big parts, studying Shakespeare made all the difference in the world. The English actors have it all over us because they've got all those wonderful companies where the actors learn to do the really big things. When I was a kid we had no such companies at all; now they're springing up all over the place. Yesterday there was no place to develop, to learn, except doing what Broadway or summer stock offered (and not many of those offerings were too exciting).

People wonder why Spencer and Jimmy Cagney and all those really great actors came out here to Hollywood and just sat. First of all, they came out because it was pleasant. They liked the sun and thought, "Oh, boy, this is great." Now, they were all hardworking actors. They'd come up the hard way, in the theater, and it was a great relief to come out here because this business is really fifty times easier. This business is an absolute cinch. You can call the studio and say, "I've got a toe-ache," and you don't have to go in. Everybody is enormously kind, forever saying, "Can't I get you a chair?" In the theater nobody does a goddam thing for you. When I saw those people yesterday give wonderful performances in *Man of LaMancha,* I thought, "My God, they've got to come on and do it all over again in four hours." Horrifying. Tough work.

Do you find any difference in the satisfaction you derive from working in the theater and in pictures?

KATHARINE HEPBURN: No, I don't think so. You see, I'm so egotistical that I have to please myself first and foremost. If I feel I've really played a scene well I'm very happy. But if I don't feel I've played it well I'm rather miserable, no matter what anyone might say to the contrary. So all the applause, while it's very nice (and certainly better than hissing), doesn't add to my satisfaction if I don't feel I was as good as I should have been.

I say this to Kathy all the time: "It's got to be great. You've got to aim for the top of the mountain because you'll never get a quarter of the way up in any event. There are just too many things in the way. But if you're perfectly satisfied just to please the director, if you don't set a really high standard for yourself, you're never going to be very interesting because people are perfectly content to have you get off at a way station. They couldn't care less."

The only person who cares is yourself. And the only way to keep going, to make anything interesting, is to set a really high standard for yourself.

In conversation on the set I've heard you describe some people as "interesting," others as "fascinating." How would you define the two words?

KATHARINE HEPBURN: I think an interesting person is someone who is enormously knowledgeable and absorbs my attention and knows a great deal that I don't and with whom I agree just enough. I find that people I don't agree with are not interesting, but irritating.

A fascinating person, to me, is someone with even

more—with personal qualities I never expected to find. I'm led up the various alleyways of their nature to find things I never expected to see, and they fill me with wonder. It's a real thrill. They are unique, and anything unique is exciting.

To turn to your career as an actress. Do you have any conscious sense of obligation to any quarter?

KATHARINE HEPBURN: I feel a definite obligation to the studio. I feel, if you accept money for something, you've got to do your best. Always. I have to be on time—it makes me enormously uncomfortable to have people wait for me. I don't care about waiting for other people, either. I organize things very carefully—don't dawdle over my makeup. I watch what the make-up men do, practice it a few times, then I can do it myself. And if there's no one around to do my hair I can do it.

I do a great deal of homework, in an odd sort of way. With this film I did two kinds of work, didn't I? I tried to help Kathy with what I felt were the possibilities of the part; when you're a kid you need help, and I always got help from marvelous sources. Then I did my own work.

In this instance, of course, I didn't work on the script because the script was almost perfect. I have, when things went sour, worked on a script. This interests me, enormously, even though it's difficult.

I love to act, and it seems ungrateful for me to loathe getting dressed up to do it. I like to rehearse, but doing it in costume is agony. I don't demand an audience; I just like to know whether or not I can pull something off.

I think I've made a great mistake—as some point I decided that the audience was my natural enemy. Perhaps it was with *The Lake,* when I made a perfect ass of myself. With that play I suffered (and may still be suffering from) a severe case of shellshock. It was a disaster, and it was my fault. First I was miscast. I don't even know whether or not I had any interpretation, but I gave a lousy performance. I had become a big star, and I went back to the stage to do *The Lake* for a very modest salary and, as I said, it was a disaster.

I think it may be a key to a lot of my love of privacy, my strangeness, because I don't remember being frightened of an audience before I did that play. And being afraid of an audience has, since then, played a major part in my life. The first night I could feel the audience wanting to like me; the kid who'd made four smash-hit movies, this wonderful and fascinating character. But the whole thing was so bad I could feel their liking and their interest recede, like one of those terrible dinner parties where the conversation just dies. The notices, which I wouldn't read, were horrible, I'm told. Not a kind word from anyone. One or two critics thought I was terribly nervous, and pardoned me to some extent, but it was awful.

On the second night a woman came backstage and said, "You're in a lot of trouble," and I said, "Yes, I am. Who are you?" She said, "I'm a teacher." "Do you want to teach me?" I asked. She said, "Yes, I do. I think I can help you." So I said, "No question about my needing help. What we have to do is work all day, then you watch the play at night and we'll go home and discuss it." That's the way I did *The Lake*. Finally I was giving a good performance in the thing, but I was twenty years too young to play the part. We paid back the expense, but it was a frightening experience, and it made me terrified of the public. This is a shame because they aren't out there waiting to choke you; they're hoping for you, they want to be with you, they don't want to see you fall down. They're enormously kind, but after *The Lake* they've terrified me.

Obligations—there are so many. To the studio, who's putting a fortune into it. (It's a shame that films here cost so damned much to make.) To your costars and your directors and the writer. To everyone. This is why nothing but the best you can do is even remotely acceptable, because you can never do quite enough.

I'd like to go back to some of the other subjects we've touched on. For example, several times in the past weeks you've referred to the fact that the woman is still a second-class citizen. Could you elaborate on that?

KATHARINE HEPBURN: I feel certain that a woman's *position* is that of a second-class citizen, but how she can avoid this I don't know. It may be an absolute necessity. I know that if a mother is not at home, available to the child, the childs is apt to become very insecure. I know that when I realized I was going to lead a professional life, to become a victim of what I did, I very quickly decided I would never have any children.

You see, I had been the result of a family who had been at home. I'd had a very conventional upbringing. Mother did a lot, but the things she did never interfered with us. I think a lot of women do a great deal without neglecting their children, but if they're really involved in a career, out competing with men, it bloody well does interfere with the children. It has to. It certainly interferes with the normal relationship with the husband, because if you've got two people out there the woman can say, "*You're* tired; what about me?"

The male, ideally, built up as the king of the castle, becomes intimidated if his position is threatened. He's the king only because he's not at home so much, but when both parents are preoccupied with a career his position is tenuous.

I don't know. Considering the overpopulation problem I think the woman who has a career should have a career. I think a person has to make up his or her mind in life; I don't think you can have everything. If a woman is going to have a career she should not, by and large, have children, because the children are just the goats. The real responsibility is to bring children up, not to just have them, isn't it? I think women get stuck with the frightfully tough decision in these cases —they always do—but they can't be sentimental about it.

For example, I've seen actresses who have children who are absolutely tormented when the children are ill, and they can't stay with them because the show must be done or the movie must be made; they go through hell. They don't know what to do, so the children have to rely on someone else because the person who is there is the person the children rely on, the mother or the nurse or whomever. Whoever is with them is the person they depend upon and love.

In many instances I think it would be better if the woman worked and the man stayed at home. I don't think it matters *who* stays at home, as long as it's one of them. Nurses and housekeepers and baby-sitters may be fine, perfectly splendid, but they don't have the continuation, the tenure, a parent has.

What is your attitude toward divorce? Both in terms of legal aspects and popular practice?

KATHARINE HEPBURN: Well, I don't particularly believe in marriage. I think it's an artificial relationship because you have to sign a contract. I think it's a relationship which is only a guarantee made for the sake of the children, in hopes that the children will have a good solid foundation.

I don't think the male and female necessarily need the arrangement, it certainly doesn't keep them together anymore. You can't ask two people who are totally disinterested in each other to live together because it's cruel. It's not normal.

I think people often dive into marriage without knowing what the hell they're doing nor who the hell they're committing themselves to. I think I'd feel slightly silly if I'd been married four or five times—"Come, come, my dear, make up your mind," you know.

Obviously, you have to have divorce. The whole procedure of divorce is a mess, however. In very Catholic countries the woman is the goat; the man can build up a relationship on the side and come off scot-free, but if the woman builds up the same sort of relationship the man can take all the children, which is ridiculous because the children really belong with the mother. She is obviously better suited to care for them, and more interested in them than the man. Maybe they'd all behave better if they weren't tied to each other. Who the hell knows?

I'm not even sure that men and women suit each other enough to live in the same house. I really don't think so. I think women get on very nicely with other women—they have the same interests. My women friends are much more relaxing to me than men. Men you've got to wait on and look respectable for, and my way of dressing isn't exactly calculated to please men. I usually look like the ragpicker's daughter. But I'm not a woman who has liked men, as a sex. Men with a capital M. I like individual men, but I like women, on the whole, better. I think they're much more admirable as characters. Much better friends. God knows they have to put up with a lot, but they still keep a sense of humor about themselves, something most men don't really have.

I'm mad about that book about Picasso, written by his mistress. She had a sense of humor about herself, but men have practically none of this same sort of humor. I don't think they could live the way they do if they had one. But I like husbands and fathers and beaus; I think they're fine. But not as a steady diet. They require a great deal of effort. In the course of living I can't put up with that much.

On my final day in Hollywood I watched Katharine Hepburn play tennis. Then we went for a drive in the mountains surrounding the reservoir.

Everything she had said so often, about her philosophy of life being found in her game of tennis, was true.

"You've got to keep the ball in front of you, never behind—reach out—follow through," she explained between sets. The sun was bright on the Beverly Hills Hotel tennis courts. Her opponent, the top pro at the hotel, had just been illegitimately beaten by Katharine. She was hot, perspiring, but not tired.

She lost the second set by a narrow margin. As I watched her I totally forgot about the word "age." On the courts she ran with the grace and fluidity of a sixteen-year-old girl. Her service was powerful. When she missed a shot an expletive was followed by a terse, "Get behind it, slow leg."

She lost a third set, then went to shower and dress. The white tennis shorts were exchanged for the (inevitable) tan slacks, the moribund sweater, the scarf, the cap, the fatigue jacket. This time, however, the slacks were not neatly pressed. They were stained and creaseless and one leg was torn from above the ankle to just above the knee.

"Brambles," she explained. "You really can't walk around up at the reservoir without tearing everything."

She untied Dog—a small, cream-colored German shepherd—from a tree near the courts. Then we drove to the reservoir.

As we climbed the canyon drive, she slowed to point out a small white house set back from the road. "This is where I lived when I came out here, in 1932. Nice little house, nice middle-class neighborhood. My friend Laura Harting and I discovered the reservoir when we used to take her dogs for walks, way back then, so you might say that the reservoir has been an important part of my life for thirty-five years."

We entered the reservoir enclosure, almost five hundred acres of uncleared mountain slopes that surround a large, deep lake. All this, five minutes away from the Beverly Hills Hotel.

We stopped at the crest of a steep hill. Dog climbed out and started to rummage through the underbrush, spurting to a gallop when he spotted a ground squirrel. Katharine and I climbed a few feet down the slope and began to pick nasturtiums from an enormous wild bed.

"Years ago, somebody threw plants or seeds out here, and look what's happened." The flowers were so thick it was almost impossible not to step on them. The blossoms themselves were enormous, variegated in mixtures of orange, yellow, and red that no seed catalog can promise. The endless growing season of

Southern California had worked miracles. "Love these flowers," she commented. "The spicy smell. Nothing phony about them. They were my mother's favorite."

We put the bouquets in the back seat and drove on. Dog galloped ahead, stopping occasionally to chase some unseen animal down a slope. Katharine would stop the car until he returned.

"Two splendid blue herons live right up there," she said at one point. "I'm sorry they're not out for you. Beautiful birds." She sat back. "This is lovely, isn't it? So much like New England. I think I'd have gone mad out here if it hadn't been for this place. Too bad it's so filled with poison oak. All those beautiful, glossy green leaves are murderous. I know. I'm California's best customer for yellow kitchen soap."

We sat for awhile and looked at the lake. Dog came back to check the car, then ran farther down toward the water.

"We flushed a deer at this point, last fall. Poor animal. Dog startled it, and it leaped a fence. The fence was only four feet on this side, but the drop on the other side was ten feet, and the the deer landed on its chest. We had to kill it. Terrible.

Again the silence, punctuated only by birdsong.

"You saw me play tennis. I think I play well enough though I'm really 'the privileged class enjoying its privileges'—spoonfed. But you know life is like that game. You've got to think ahead. You've got to be aggressive because if you don't move ahead you slip behind. Nobody stands still. In a career. In life. So get behind it and shove—that's the way to get it out of the mud—lean forward."

Dog returned and Katharine opened a rear door to let him in. She pressed the button to bring the top back over the convertible and I locked it.

"You've got to be aggressive, you've got to stay ahead, but sometimes you've got to find peace." She looked at the lake, at the wind-ruffled trees and bushes that screened the shoreline.

"All for free."

Sidney Poitier

THE NEGRO actor has always had difficulty finding a place in the American theater. Racial prejudice has played its restrictive role in all but the major cities of the North. But even on Broadway and in cities like Chicago and San Francisco, there is bigotry. (I am not referring, here, to the various musical fields; as vocalist or instrumentalist the Negro has come into his own, though not without difficulty and perhaps without problems still in existence. We are speaking here of the "straight" actor.)

As restrictive as the issue of whether or not the Negro is allowed to act is the problem of what he can act *in*. Few plays, whether classical or contemporary, include good roles for Negroes. Since audiences are still prone to judge the Negro actor as a Negro first, then as an actor, it is difficult to integrate the cast of a play by casting a Negro in a basically "white" part. Plays have been written, of course, for all-Negro casts, and "white" plays have been played by all-Negro casts, but the former have not been produced frequently enough, and the latter become Negro theater, which is another matter entirely.

The same restrictions apply to Hollywood, though in the past few decades considerable progress has been made. Sammy Davis, Jr. has scored in straight roles, the late Dorothy Dandridge shone in *Island in the Sun,* and Godfrey Cambridge has made the most of meaty parts. Towering over all of them, however—firmly placed at the very peak of the acting profession as a whole—stands Sidney Potier.

Guess Who's Coming to Dinner is Poitier's twenty-third film. It does not contain the violence and impact which made *The Defiant Ones* memorable, nor the extreme emotional stress that dominated *In the Heat of the Night* and *To Sir, With Love. Guess Who's Coming to Dinner* is, however, factual in many respects and it is sensitive. It requires an actor of Poitier's caliber, and a romantic aura that requires Sidney Poitier, period. For whatever else must be said in praise of Poitier's talents, one very physical fact cannot be ignored: He is one of the handsomest men at work today—tall, broad-shouldered, and slim-hipped. He has a great—and frequent—laugh, and a presence that commands attention.

Watching him, listening to him, week after week, permits one to dig beneath the surface. Here resides an enormously complex man who might be difficult to get to know, but infinitely worth every effort. His fund of sensitivity and intelligence is obvious to all who have watched him in films. Not so apparent on the screen is an inner restlessness, a tendency to brood, an insistence upon absolute truth. Stanley Kramer's assertion that Sidney stands at the peak of his profession, and at the head of his race, is probably based upon this search for truth.

I observed Sidney as he blew the work of an entire morning because a certain line did not ring true; he could not fit the words into the mouth of the physician he portrayed and pressed to have it rewritten. (Stanley Kramer obliged.)

For several days he debated whether or not he would appear at the Academy Award presentations, since he was the only Negro originally scheduled, and he felt his race's representation too meager. Diahann Carroll was added, and Sidney appeared.

With Sidney one watches words very carefully or learns to. Do not use "angry" when you merely mean "annoyed," or "love" when you mean "admire." Sidney quickly digs to the root of what you intended to say, and he can make you feel like a damned fool—not because he intends to paint you the fool, but because he wants things precisely understood.

He provides an invaluable experience for any writer who tends to use words carelessly.

Guess Who's Coming to Dinner marks a notable reunion between Kramer and Poitier. Sidney gained recognition as a major film star in *The Defiant Ones* which Stanley produced in 1958. He was nominated for an Academy Award for *The Defiant Ones* and won the award for *Lilies of the Field*. Sidney is probably at his peak, both as to techincal ability and popularity.

Like costars Spencer Tracy and Katharine Hepburn, Sidney Poitier is one of those actors who sincerely dislikes to talk about himself and his profession. But toward the end of my stay in Hollywood, he did tape an extended and satisfying session that is best broken into subjects.

For example, I asked him if he regarded New York as home.

SIDNEY POITIER: I don't have a home. I live in the world. A home has never been important to me. I've lived in a shack most of my life because my parents were poor. My father could never afford more than a couple of rooms. Three rooms was the largest he ever had, and that was at the height of the family unit. We were six boys, two girls.

This was in the Bahamas, and I lived in that kind of complex until I was about fourteen. Then I came to America. I lived in hovels, one room here, one room there, so when I came to adulthood I hadn't the experience of living in a home, the sort of place we in affluent America understand as the generally accepted concept of a home.

Houses, places, have never meant much to me, so I don't really live anywhere. I live where I'm loved, and when I was a kid I had a lot of people around who were interesting people, caring people, and a lot of friends. There was a texture of love and warmth in the communities in which I lived when I was a kid in the Caribbean, so I seek that still, more than I seek a place of shelter. Today I have an apartment in New York. My children live in Pleasantville, New York, in a big house with their mother. I rent quarters in California, and I'm building a house in the Caribbean. But I don't have a home. I find New York a home sometimes, the West Indies at others, London or Hollywood or wherever I'm working when I'm there.

How did you happen to leave the West Indies?

SIDNEY POITIER: When I was about thirteen or fourteen my father was unable to exercise much discipline over me. I was the last of the children; the others were pretty well grown, and I was the baby. At fourteen I was incorrigible, and he was getting on in years because he'd had me when he was forty-three. It was difficult for him to once again have to deal with an adolescent, so I ran wild in Nassau. I had a friend who went to reform school, and my father was afraid I'd end up the same way. So my father decided that, because I was born in Florida (my parents had gone to Miami to sell produce in 1927 when my mother was seven or eight months pregnant, and they wouldn't let her go back, so I was born in Florida), he could get me out of the Caribbean because of my American citizenship. By then I had a brother living in Florida, and my father wrote to him and told him his dilemma, that there was no hope for me in the Bahamas, that he had to get me out of there. He had no money, and asked my brother if he would undertake the responsibility of salvaging me from a scene where he felt I'd only get to reform school. I most likely would have, too, if I'd remained. I was a strange kid, not rough, just weird. I did a lot of odd things.

Anyway, my father and mother and oldest brother conspired to get me out of the Caribbean, and they did it.

How did you become an actor?

SIDNEY POITIER: I went on to New York, still very young, and I used to wash dishes and do odd jobs. I worked mostly in hotel or restaurant kitchens because I could earn a salary plus my meals. I used to find these jobs in the papers.

One time I was between jobs and going through a Negro newspaper, *The Amsterdam News,* and next to the want-ad section was the theatrical section, and on that page it said "Actors wanted." It looked just like "Dishwashers wanted" just across from it, so I figured what the hell, I'd give it a whirl.

I went to the address listed (I was sixteen or seventeen), to a little theater in Harlem, and a guy said to me, "Are you an actor?" and I said, "Of course." He said. "Where have you studied?" and I said "Everywhere." Then he said, "Okay, go up on the stage and read page such-and-such from this script." So I went up and I couldn't read. I was terrible. And he very impatiently dragged me off the stage and threw me out on my bottom. When we came to the door, he said, "Look, boy, don't waste our time. You're no actor and you can't ever be one. Go get a job and forget about acting. It's not for you."

Well, this presented me with a challenge, and I decided that if I didn't become an actor I'd forever be what he said, essentially worthless, useless. So I said to myself, "If I'm ever to be anything in life I will have to become an actor and show him that I can avoid being what he said I'd be." Actually, I set out to do something I really had no great interest in. I just wanted to prove to him and to myself that there was more than met his eye.

I bought a radio for fourteen dollars and started listening to it because he told me that I spoke terribly. I had a horrible West Indian accent, and there's no place in the theater for that accent. I listened to the radio every night for six months, from the time I got home from work until I went to sleep, and I repeated every sound I heard. I succeeded in changing my speech, not altogether, but quite noticeably.

Then I went back and asked for an audition at that theater, and after a whole lot of debate they accepted me as a student. That's how I got my start. (I guess it wasn't a bad try for a kid whose formal education was a bit limited; I started school at eleven and quit at twelve and a half.)

I worked very hard at that theater, but I was very shy and had terrible inhibitions. My speech was an inhibiting factor, so I didn't participate as much as I should have. I worked by myself, at home, but within a year I got a job as an actor in Broadway theater. I wasn't ready for it, and the play only lasted four days, but I got very good reviews. More or less by accident.

I kept working, but it wasn't until a few years later that I decided I wanted to learn the business, really learn the craft. Then I decided that I wanted to be the best actor in the world. I figured that I'd found something that gave me great satisfaction, an opportunity to find a better self-image, and I was going to stay with it and work with it, which I did. It wasn't that I was aware of any special gifts or qualities. I've always been aware of my inadequacies, my shortcomings, and have tried to strengthen myself by eliminating the shortcomings. So most of my work, most of my energies, have gone into weeding out the weaknesses.

You asked me once why I don't drink or smoke. It's just that they aren't essential to me. I can only speak in terms of my own needs, my own personality, but they aren't essential. I tried drinking. I tried smoking. The state of being up on alcohol or down on cigarettes is not necessarily the state I prefer. I prefer to be sober. Being sober is a state, just like being high on pot is a state. I elect for the sober state because I am more in control of my sensitivities, more in control of my awareness, and my sensitivities and awareness are related to the objective reality. I don't want the objective reality colored by the influence of booze or pot.

I also believe that the artist has a responsibility. Each artist is born with a gift. It's a gift that does not belong to him. It's a gift he hasn't paid for, hasn't earned, nothing he has cultivated or engineered as a result of his own choice. Something happened at the moment of conception; inherent in the seed was this gift. The nature of the life he lived, of the many, many external circumstances in this life, contributed toward agitating and irritating this seed, and by the time the person became a young adult the gift came to fruition.

I consider such a gift to be more than the exclusive property of the artist in whom it's found, just as I consider a pearl to be more than the exclusive property of the oyster. So it's the artist's responsibility not to use the gift selfishly, but to use it, to husband it, to care for it, to nurture it, for mankind. It belongs to everybody because people come to him and ask him to share it. He shares it, and they go away feeling as though they have partaken of something that has done for them what they, themselves, couldn't do.

As I say, this is only my point of view, and I've got to regard it as truth. If it is true, then the artist has the responsibility of taking very good care of the house in which his gift resides. His body and mind are the tools of his craft. He needs them and must employ them, so they should be kept in good working order. It is in this context that I believe drinking and smoking are an abuse of the body. Not that I am an absolute abstainer; on occasion I will have a glass of wine and, once in a great while, a shot.

Why is it you don't like to talk about acting?

SIDNEY POITIER: When I became an actor—especially after I came into the movie industry—I found that there is a tendency to denigrate actors. Not just the public, but a lot of people in the business resent the attention actors get, and for a while I resented being an actor.

This craft is tenuous; the potentiality of it, the fragility of it, the fantasty of it. It isn't easy to stand up and make a militant defense of fantasy. It makes you feel like an idiot. You're a man, and you get older, and you're still called to defend fantasies. This is what the actor must always contend with; the vulnerability, the undefendability. When the function doesn't succeed, it's hard to know where to direct the anger—at the business, for doing the wrong thing, or at yourself, for not having the proper strength to resist doing the wrong thing. There are so many alternatives and so many rewards along each alternate road.

The money makes it confusing sometimes. The definition of what is "popular" makes it confusing. The need to express yourself can be complicated by trying to please someone else with that expression. Very often, in this business, the nebulous "someone" you're trying to please turns out to be a product of statistics, and the result is that you please no one because you've become impersonal.

Big business—the communications industries as a whole—has a tendency to underrate the mass audience. I think this is a terrible mistake. They underrate the individual's ability to see and appreciate something that's very personal. I think this is tragic. And I know that I do it, myself. I'm always surprised when people see a particular little truth I felt was private or hard to grasp and I say, "You mean you really saw that?" Then I think how arrogant I was to think they wouldn't see it. The audience probably sees more than I do.

I believe that the mass audience doesn't recognize the absence of something very personal and truthful but I believe they always recognize its presence.

But you see, I've got to do more than act now, and this fall I'm directing a play. Why?

I've been acting for twenty-one years. I've been very successful at the game. I've always been a person who works instinctively, and I find it a waste of time and energy to repeat, and repetition seldom breaks new ground. I have begun to repeat myself as an actor in all too many ways.

Once you become successful in this game a certain kind of image becomes the personality that is the bankable product in this industry. I'm considered to be a certain type of personality, and I'm hired more often than not for that type of role. Even though I've had great opportunity and diversity in the parts I've been offered and the parts I've accepted, I still find myself in a circle that reminds me I played this before, I played that before. So I've decided that I don't want to spend the next twenty years of my life repeating myself as a successful actor. I want a new challenge. I want to reach a bit further, extend my grasp.

The director has an enormous opportunity for expression because he has almost complete control over all the contributing forces—the actors, the writer, the set designer, the technicians, and (if it's a movie) the cinematographer. All these people are guided by him, so he weaves all these creative contributions into a total. A total that comes from his own imagination, his own concept. The style and fabric of the completed work is largely the director's and that has to be an enormous satisfaction. So I want to find out if I have the gift for direction or if I haven't, to obtain this satisfaction or forget it.

To turn to Guess Who's Coming to Dinner. *How do you feel about its importance, thematically, and about its validity?*

SIDNEY POITIER: I have no way of determining how important it will be in a racial sense. It's awfully complex and we are not in the business of addressing ourselves directly to, nor exclusively to, the racial issue. In this film we are first and foremost, it seems to me, interested in presenting entertainment with a point of view—entertainment that will first be accepted as such, then as a premise, a side of the issue. I really don't quite understand what I do think of it in racial terms.

I know there's a validity to it. It's a situation that exists in this country, exists all over the world. It exists on a racial level, on a religious level, on a class level, on an economic level. People become involved in each others' lives without much concern for peripheral considerations. What is usually the intrinsic consideration is how one person feels about the other. The peripheral considerations will most certainly ultimately influence the central feeling. But the central feeling, if it's a strong one, the really rooted initial instinctive response, is big enough to transcend those peripheral considerations.

To move to the larger picture of integration, what principles, what course of action, do you consider proper?

SIDNEY POITIER: I don't think integration can work as simply as we presuppose. We know now it is not as simple as we heretofore thought it might be. Not because people think a certain way, but because of the institutionalization of certain habit patterns, habit patterns that cannot be changed until cerain structural changes are made in the machinery that produces the human being. I'm speaking of the social procedure that produces a human being.

A twenty-five-year-old American is rather like a

product—a product coming off an assembly line designed to create a certain object. Or like the result of a recipe.

Example: You put beans in a casserole, add salt, sugar, pepper, little pieces of bacon, water. It doesn't matter how large or small the oven is, all you're going to get out of that dish is baked beans. Follow? You put a young human instrument into this socioeconomic complex we have in America, where the values are overwhelmingly in favor of pleasure and materalism, and you're going to produce an individual who is not really a purveyor or supporter or practioner or disciple of certain aesthetic, certain human, values. You cannot hate people you don't know unless you are raised in a society where your propensity for hate is cultivated.

We have a propensity for hate. We also have a propensity for love. We have a propensity for fear, and we also have a propensity for understanding. We have the capacity to embrace all the opposites as they exist in nature. They are encased in each and every one of us.

Now, a society that cultivates the love that is in us will find that love, as it emerges from the person in his daily life, spreads in the same way that hate or fear or distrust or whatever negative impulses and qualities exist now spread. Love can and should be more dominant than the negatives. I don't believe that we in the United States teach the value of the human instrument. We teach other values. Our children aren't reared on how glorious it is to be human; we don't teach the glory of the human animal. We don't teach our children the love of this incredible miracle called the human being. We teach other things that culminate in a racial division, a religious division, a class division, a lack of concern, a callousness, a disinterest in the needs of others.

I don't believe this is the way life has to be or should be. I believe that inherent in each individual in society is a positive quality of human life, and that if we devise that kind of society (or the aspect of society) that will cultivate these qualities, we would have a better society. Not until then will we have a better society in which to live.

In order to discuss integration, with this in mind, I have to depart immediately and say that I don't think integration is going to come about within the context of things as they now are. I think there has to be a gigantic change in the structure of our country—philosophically, economically, politically, sociologically. It must be!

One simple example: In order to eliminate slums you just cannot eliminate slums. You've got to cultivate people to appreciate their transfer from the slums. That cultivation alone will cost billions of dollars in adult education, in strengthening the educational system in poor communities. The job is enormous. The elimination of slums means that one hell of a lot of work has to be done with the people who live there. An extremely dimensional attack must be made to educate the slum dweller beyond the capacity he now has. Moving him isn't conditioning him or educating him.

I think we're going to have to reverse the obsession Americans have with the profit system. Don't get me wrong; I'm not putting down the profit system. I dig it. But I think that inherent in our profit system is a failure to encourage the individual to become useful to the community in ways other than making a material profit.

In other words, if a man is out of work, a black man or a white man, whose skills are insufficient or not needed in the nation's labor pool, why should he frustrate himself in the wasteland of the unemployed community? He should be of service to something, even if it's to the government. He doesn't have to necessarily work for a profit. We're now in a situation where we're going to have to find ways to employ people in areas other than profit-making organizations and corporations because the profit-making side of our industrial complex is not sufficiently elastic to absorb the entire labor pool. It can't now, and as the labor pool keeps growing, the consequent unemployment will grow worse.

I feel that a great many Americans ought to be doing useful work, but there is no place for them under the profit system. And as marvelous and magnificent as the profit system is and has been for most of us, it simply has no room for these people. We're going to have to make room for them because their numbers are going to grow.

I think that until the United States realizes that there is nothing it can do with its Negro, Oriental, Mexican, and Puerto Rican populations but create certain basic equalities of opportunity, we are not going to have much progress in integration. We're going to have only token progress.

It all boils down to a simple blunt fact. The white community is going to have to make up its mind, whether it likes it or not, to help or to suppress. Twenty million Negroes in this country are not asking for something unreasonable. They're asking for better education, better housing, and an equal chance at the good life. An *equal* chance—that is not being unreasonable. Either you help them get this equal chance or you repress them. There's no middle way at all, at all, at all.

It isn't a question of whether the Negro is going to

move next door. If open housing took place overnight there wouldn't be a rush to the white communities. The questions are more basic. Housing is important, and education is important, but I don't think the Negro can accomplish the meaningful equality by himself.

If the white world is indifferent we're going to have enormous problems in this country. Serious and terrible problems. If the white community puts a stop to the progress of twenty million Negroes and feels that the Negro has moved as far as he wants him to move as certain governors and police chiefs and right-wing organizations are saying, the Negro frustration will find no outlet and will continue to build and build and build to fierce explosions. Unfortunately, such explosions will be treated by repressive measures. One repressive measure will lead to another, and it's unthinkable, horribly unthinkable, the explosion that could come if the repression goes beyond the point of endurance.

But oh, to understand, to tolerate, to love, to enjoy—these are the things that should be taught. Not to profit and to hate.

Katharine Houghton

YOU CAN'T say, at first glance, that you *know* Katharine Houghton is Katharine Hepburn's niece. Yet after watching her over a period of weeks, on and off the set, and then seeing again such Hepburn classics as *Little Women* and *Stage Door,* you decide that you were unobservant in failing to note a resemblance which is quite striking.

Miss Houghton is beautiful: this you notice first. She is tall (though not as tall as her aunt) and has a full figure. Her complexion is light, her hair a shade midway between gold and tawny. Her face is youthful round. But when she is caught, by chance, in a shadow, or the set lighting is dimmed after a take, you instantly recall the Hepburn of *The Warrior's Husband* (Broadway) and *A Bill of Divorcement* (Hollywood). The cheekbones, the jawline, a tilt of the head, a gliding way of moving.

At the present time, Miss Houghton cannot press the

resemblance far, nor does she wish to. "I don't mind coming into this film as Katharine Hepburn's niece, but I want to come out of it as Katharine Houghton," sums up her attitude. Thus, it is probably fortunate that her face is rounded with youth, her voice pitched a bit high. Eventually, as she matures, her face will thin, her voice will drop, and the Hepburn brand of determination will accent her chin and her eyes.

But for the present she is Katharine Houghton, very much her own young woman. And that is quite enough.

KATHARINE HOUGHTON: I was born in Hartford, Connecticut, attended a girls' day school and Sarah Lawrence College. I studied voice, but I had no interest in going into the theater until I got involved in some underground films. These were purely amateur things, no more than forty minutes long, sixteen millimeter, made by students in the New York area and at Princeton. I wrote one, myself, at college, an adaptation of a medieval mystery play. But we worked hard at them, though they were done strictly for our own amusement.

I got very interested in cinematics at this point, and went to the courses in film technique at the Museum of Modern Art and saw all the old—really old—movies, virtually a history of cinematography.

At the end of my junior year at Sarah Lawrence I was faced with the first real decision acting brought—whether to take some extra courses so I could eventually go to Harvard for my Ph.D. in philosophy, or go into summer stock.

I decided in favor of summer stock at Ivoryton, Connecticut. I was purely an apprentice because I'd never done anything in professional theater, but I figured that since I was young and reasonably healthy,

I'd see what I could do. I knew I could alway go back to philosophy. (I still can.)

The interest in theater and cinematography grew, and in the spring of my senior year I auditioned for the APA. I still wasn't Equity, and they accepted me for their student program. But then their Ford Foundation grant failed to come through, so they couldn't go ahead with their student program. (Later they got the grant.) Garson Kanin was doing a play at that time, and he asked me if I wanted to audition to understudy the part of the granddaughter in his play. I got the part, and during the summer his wife, Ruth Gordon, who had adapted the play, wrote in a small part for me. The small part became the first professional thing I did. The play ran on Broadway, and my little part was wonderful because so many theater people—directors and producers, agents and casting people—saw the play, and my part got me lots of interviews and sort of opened the door to more possibilities than had existed to that point.

The next thing that happened was that I was cast as the female lead in William Inge's play, *Where's Daddy?* It was a huge part; I never left the stage. The director, Howard Clurman, thought I was great for it, even though I was inexperienced, but the producer felt shaky about me. A week before we opened he put my understudy, an older, more experienced girl, in the part. He felt he didn't dare trust me with it.

It may have been the right thing to do. If I'd had more experience I wouldn't have been nervous about it and, God knows, I was nervous. I think I could have done the part, but at the time I had no defense. I wanted to please everyone, and I did what everybody said. It was my fault because I didn't have enough experience behind me to give the impression that I was assured. I think you must do this; if you're terrified and show it, you make other people apprehensive. Anyway, I stayed on to understudy the girl who'd replaced me, but the play got terrible reviews and closed rather quickly so I never got a chance to play the part. Maybe, in retrospect, I was lucky to have gotten out of it.

After that I did a small TV spot on a program, "The Hawk," a mystery series, and I played Ophelia. It was a play-within-a-play about a Shakespearean company, and it was great fun. And in an ABC special titled "The Confession," I played the only girl in the play, a girl who was killed near the beginning. It was a dramatic, traumatic little part, but good for me, apparently, because by that time I began to feel a sort of self-confidence. I began to feel that I knew what I was doing, that I could take direction, not have direction thrown me. I could sort out what the direction meant in relation to how I felt about it instead of letting it inhibit me.

It wasn't Method. The Method type of acting simply doesn't go with my temperament. I think it's awfully contrived—on me it would certainly look contrived.

It's odd, because as a child—which I certainly was then—you want to do what you're told. As an actress, you want to do what the directors wants. Yet it has to come from you, or you're an automaton—not an actor, a puppet. This is why I think that as a very young person without experience, one of the most important things to learn is how to take direction in a way that pleases everyone—including yourself—and give a good performance. If you're an old pro this is no problem at all, but someone who's starting out, who lacks self-confidence, who doesn't know what they're like or what their potential is, their weak spots, their strong spots, finds it difficult to know how much to rely on what someone says, or how to follow (intellectually) what they are saying. In the process of walking over to that table to pick up that glass and bring it over here, you have to let your instincts tell you how to do it. You can't just do it mechanically, without making it part of the concept of the character.

After doing the last ABC special for TV I met Stanley Kramer in New York. My aunt had wanted me to meet him for a long time because he and Spencer were such close friends. He'd passed through New York several times, but we'd never managed to meet. But one day when I was auditioning for a medieval play—I had on a sort of dirndl, and my hair in two long braids—she called and said, "Go over to the Plaza in ten minutes because Mr. Kramer's there and he's on his way to Europe, but you might just be able to catch him to say 'Hello.'" I had no idea that anything more than sociability was involved because Aunt Kat had wanted me to meet Stanley Kramer the same way she'd introduced me to George Cukor and other people who are her close friends.

So I went over and said, "How do you do," and he very graciously asked me to sit for awhile, and did I want ginger ale or something, and we ended up talking for three and one half hours. Curiously enough, we talked about the underground films and the scenarios I was writing, and he told me about how, when he was young, he'd started a film repertory group. I told him how this had been one of my dreams. Finally he said, "You know, I'm going to start a new film. May I tell you about it?" I said, "Certainly," (still not having the faintest idea that I could be involved) and he told me the whole story with animation and enthusiasm. I'll never forget it. He was like a small child, gloriously excited, as he told it.

Then he said, "Guess who's going to play the newspaperman, the father? Spencer Tracy." I said, "Wonderful! Spencer is going to make another movie!" He said,

"Guess who's going to play the mother? Katharine Hepburn." All I could say was "Wonderful!" which was the way I felt; I'd heard nothing at all about this from Aunt Kat. He said, "Guess who's going to play the doctor? Sidney Poitier." I said, "Wow, what a group!"

But he didn't say, "Guess who's going to play the daughter," and I hadn't the slighest idea he had me in mind, so we talked about those three stars for awhile and finally he said, "Do you think you could do the part of the girl?" I said, "I don't know because I really don't know what it would entail, but if you ever want me to do a reading for you I'd be glad to." With a talky script like this I think you can get a damned good idea as to whether someone could do the part just from having them do a reading.

This was all that was said about the part, and I left. About a month later everything descended upon me at once. I was offered two films, two good TV programs, and a possible repertory engagement. I had a terrible choice to make as to what to do. The television was tempting because of the money involved, but my heart said, "Do the theater because you'll learn infinitely more." As I was in the process of making the decision (by then I'd boiled it down to television or repertory), I received a barrage of phone calls from my agents saying, "Don't get involved for six months with anything, because there's a possibility, a faint possibility, that Stanley Kramer may want you for his film." I kept saying, "Oh, come on, this is nonsense, absolute nonsense," but they said, "No, it isn't, he's really interested." So I said, "Give me his number and I'll call him and ask him." They were shocked and said, "Oh, you can't do that!" But I replied, "We had such a nice meeting in August I feel I could do it, and that he'd give me a direct answer."

I had felt, in Stanley Kramer, a directness and an honesty; if somebody asked him a question he'd give them a direct answer; that he wouldn't be offended if I said, "What would you advise me to do? I have a choice to make. Would you advise me to do the repertory or the TV?" Finally, they gave me his number and I called him and said, "I've been told that you're possibly, remotely, considering me to test for your film and I have a decision to make. If I could choose the TV it will take me through June, and I couldn't possibly be considered by you, but if I do the repertory, I could." He said, "Do the repertory." I said, "That's all I want to know. Thank you very much."

I went to New Orleans where I did *Charley's Aunt*—I played the part of the ingenue. It was great fun, and I think I learned a great deal down there; we must have given seventy-five performances. We also took scenes around to various schools to perform; it was a government project. We did Shakespeare and other classic plays—in scenes only, of course. But I felt the experience filled in a lot of gaps in my training, in my background, and I gained a sense of security, a sense of confidence, regarding my own instincts. In the theater you can experiment with the audience by trying scenes and lines and gestures different ways, but you are really experimenting with yourself. And you also learn so very, very much from other actors, more experienced actors. So, regardless of Stanley Kramer's part in my future, it was the right choice to have made.

I had planned to stay in New Orleans an extra week, just to see the next show open, but again I received a barrage of phone calls from my agents. I hadn't heard a word about *Guess Who's Coming to Dinner* all this time. I thought, "Well, he's forgotten. He's gotten some glamorous, famous creature to play the part." But now they were saying, "Hurry back to New York. You can't get here fast enough." So I flew back the day we closed the play, and Stanley Kramer was in town for a week, staying again at the Plaza Hotel. I went over and he said, "I'd like you to read this. Come back tomorrow and audition for me." He gave me a copy of the script, and I read it and loved it. I was so moved I could only think, "God, if I can do this!"

I went back the next day at one o'clock and I must have read for him for an hour and fifteen minutes. He said, "Just relax and start from the beginning. Read everybody's part, and do just what you want to do. Pretend I'm not here, and work on the script the way you would if you were alone. Just give me an idea of what this girl is like. I don't have any definite idea in my mind, so give me a few ideas."

I read, and we talked about various things, about how important it was for the girl to look young, yet have enough maturity to make it believable that an eminent doctor like Sidney Poitier would fall in love with her. She couldn't be a kid; she had to have an element of maturity that would interest an older man. But no definite word from Stanley.

Later I talked to Aunt Kat, and she said, "What do you think? How do you think it went?" and I said, "I have no idea. I read, and we talked about it, and he was very nice, but nothing definite, like 'You have the part' or 'Congratulations' was said. So we'll just see what happens."

On Wednesday Stanley went back to the Coast and called Aunt Kat about something (nothing to do with me) and she said, "What about little Kate? How did she do?" And he said, "What are you two? A couple of idiots?" She said, "What do you mean?" and he said, "Well, naturally, she has the part." So Aunt Kat called me, and that's the way it was. One moment in absolute hell, the next moment wondering how I could get myself to Hollywood fast enough for a press conference Stanley had scheduled for us.

What are your future ambitions as an actress? What sort of path would you like to follow? What parts do you want to play?

KATHARINE HOUGHTON: In films—well, first of all I'd like to see a renaissance in American film-making. I think so much can be done with film that isn't being done. So many technical things that aren't being done, and that can't be done in theater. The camera can go anywhere, including into the minds of people, whereas on the stage you're limited to what you can physically portray.

I'd love to be associated with a sort of repertory film group of serious professional, disciplined people who made films. We'd have writers, musicians, and so forth, and we'd do original scripts. Basing one, for instance, on the *Symphonie Fanastique,* others on certain poems, like the *Song of Roland.* Doing these things in a manner that could only only be done on film. (You can do *Hamlet* on stage or screen, but you can't do a stage version of the *Symphonie Fantastique.)* I've always been interested in doing intricate, abstract things with film that haven't been done before.

On a less quixotic level, I would like to do very interesting films involving what you might call human interest stories—good, solid prose material—such as *Guess Who's Coming to Dinner*—stories with weight, not just adventures. I'm interested in things that have something to say. On the other hand, I'm interested in a script that's highly amusing. I thought *Some Like It Hot* was wonderful and interesting. I don't know if

I'm cut out to do that type of farcical comedy, but I want to try everything.

I don't want to limit myself to being a certain type of actress. To me the most important thing is to have good people involved in a film—good writers, good technicians, good directors, good actors. Then you're bound to come up with good parts in good pictures. That, in itself, should avoid limiting myself to certain type of parts. And it would be wonderful to have free rein, to avoid getting bogged down by all the financial hindrances in this business.

I think one of the problems with films in this country is that they're so terribly costly to make. Risks can't be taken, therefore the industry tries to find scripts that are very salable. But it doesn't seem necessary to be so "safe" any more. For instance, in New York you see huge lines of people who are going to see the art films, and the films that break out of the mold. This must be good box office.

As for theater, I would love to become good enough to do well in the classics. Greek tragedy through Shakespeare, Restoration comedy, Ibsen, Strindberg, O'Neill. I love the classics, and I feel that a good stage production of any of the classics is thrilling. I think that the theater is really a place of magic because what you do in the theater is only for the present, and once it's performed it's gone forever. It vanishes into thin air, and this ephemeral quality of the theater is very fascinating to me. Also, theater is so real; you're not separated from your audience as you are in film. There's something exciting about the contact with the audience, particularly when you work with the beautiful language and the structure of the classic plays.

You said, one day on the set, that you weren't adverse to coming into the film as Katharine

Hepburn's niece, but that you wanted to come out of it as Katharine Houghton. What prompted that statement?

KATHARINE HOUGHTON: I think that when you're related to someone as great and wonderful as Aunt Kat is (and she's terrific in this profession as well as being terrific as a person), that you face a grave danger. You see, you can be given, through them, a certain opportunity. They can introduce you to people and give advice. But the danger is that you become known only because of them or associated exclusively with them. So while it's a tremendous asset, on the one hand, it's also a tricky thing to handle, particularly as far as publicity is concerned.

Ever since I got into this business people have been trying to interview me for magazines *because* I'm Katharine Hepburn's niece, so I've developed a format letter I've sent around saying, "If you promise that you will not mention Katharine Hepburn, I would be happy to give you an interview." Needless to say, nobody has ever written back, and as a consequence I didn't give out any publicity until this picture came along. (I did a little bit for the Kanin play, just newspaper photos and some tiny thing in *Newsweek.)* The reason for this is that I think it's damaging if you haven't done enough things to let people know you as yourself.

In New York very few people knew I was Katharine Hepburn's niece; I never told anybody. But out here they know because of the publicity mills of the film industry. And it was satisfying on the stage, going for auditions, getting parts without anyone knowing who I was. I knew I was being judged for myself.

But I would feel there was no point in continuing my career if people didn't know me for myself. That's why I want to come out of the film as Katharine Houghton.

What has it been like, having Katharine as an aunt?

KATHARINE HOUGHTON: Well, she's simply one of the most marvelous people I've ever met. She's amazing. First of all, she has the discipline of a Spartan soldier. She absolutely concentrates on what she's doing, and she doesn't dissipate her energy. I think she's been this way from the time she started out, and I think this accounts for a great deal of her success. Many people have talent, but they get so caught up in all sorts of things that when they're doing a film or a play they can't concentrate totally upon it.

But Aunt Kat is the perfect Descartian. She takes something and divides it into so many pieces, then divides those pieces and sets them up in a certain order and slowly reassembles them, studying them from all angles. This is the way she approaches a part. She doesn't just read her part; she has an idea of the total, of the whole, of what and which and where it is concerned.

I think it's very unusual for an actress to have such a direct, total point of view toward the entire project, yet be able to take a small section of it which is the actor's own part, and concentrate on it.

I think that in our working together on this film she has taught me how to approach a part; what one can bring to it as an individual, not in the Method sense of going through to dredge up emotional associations, but what one can, as an individual, imbue the part *with,* so that it isn't flat, a matter of lines. You can have mental associations while saying a particular thing so that it has fire and life and intensity and energy and yet be in context with everything else that is going on.

Aunt Kat has made me aware of doing scenes within a context, remaining true to the character, maintaining a firm grip upon what the character is thinking about all the time, whether she has lines or not. I've found a tangible lifeline all the way through the character I play. I feel that each scene I play has a reality, and that the reality is in context with all the other scenes. It would be possible (and thank heavens my aunt and Stanley Kramer have taught me to avoid that!) to bring reality to the scenes and have them *not* in context. Then I'd be awful, and I certainly wouldn't help the film.

How has your family felt about your aspirations as an actress?

KATHARINE HOUGHTON: My father has alway been interested in films. He makes documentary films, himself, and as a young boy he came out here and worked as a cameraman for John Ford, as an apprentice, so he's always been interested in this and he thinks it's great. I think my mother was a little apprehensive at first, but now she's all for it. Perhaps because I seem to be putting myself on solid ground.

Was Katharine Hepburn always close to you, as a person?

KATHARINE HOUGHTON: Yes, although I think that we've gotten to know each other much better since I've been out here. She was always so busy, so rushed; she'd breeze in for Christmas or Thanksgiving and the various holidays, sometimes for a week or so in summer, and it seemed she was was always breezing right off again. So as a child I saw her frequently but never got to know her well. Now, of course we're together a great deal.

What do you think the reactions to Guess Who's Coming to Dinner, *will be?*

KATHARINE HOUGHTON: It's awfully difficult for me to try to assess them because I've always been raised liberally. To me, something like this is not a shock, but I can imagine, from what I know about the South (and a hell of a lot of the North), that some people will go through the roof.

Fortunately, it isn't what you'd call a civil rights film. It isn't pointing the finger at bigotry and saying, "See how wrong you are." It's a film that tells a story about certain people, and I think it makes every effort not to become preachy. I don't feel as though its purpose is to educate, but to depict a situation that involves very outstanding people. It so happens that some of these people are white and some are Negro, but what difference does it make? It isn't showing a conflict between the races as a confrontation of humanitarian ideas, because there is no conflict. Two people are in love with each other, and they want to get married. The trouble their relationship causes is in the sphere of the emotional reactions of people who are intellectually for liberalism. It's sort of a last step before liberalism becomes an emotional reality, not just a concept. And Matt Drayton is the symbol of the 1930's, a very left-wing avant-grade liberal who believes that all men are equal and should have equal opportunity (very Marxist). Not subversive, but socialistic and humanitarian. Anyway, he's been going around all his life as a newspaper publisher, championing the underdog, and suddenly he's faced not with the underdog but with a Negro, Dr. Prentice, who is an eminent man in his own right. And he's faced with the emotional problem of accepting him as his son. He can accept him as his brother, but as his son?

This is what makes it interesting and far from trite. I think it's easy to accept certain principles until you are tested by reality; then reexamination is necessary. No doubt Matt Drayton would have invited Martin Luther King and Stokely Carmichael to dinner, and he would have been instrumental in founding an Urban League and in fighting for civil rights. But his is an intellectual liberalism that people of his generation grew up in.

My generation—we don't think of it in intellectual terms. The fact that whites and Negroes and Orientals are on an equal level has been absorbed by us. We look at people as people, and I think this is very true of all my friends. We don't notice nationalities or colors. My three best girl friends are, respectively, German, Chinese, and an American. But I know them so well as people that they're never a color or a nationality; they are simply wonderful, valuable people and loyal friends. I think the difference in the generations of liberals shows up in the scene where Matt Drayton talks to Dr. Prentice, and says, "Well, Dr. Prentice, we've talked about many things, but what about having children?" And he says, "Mr. Drayton, I—we've talked about it and we're going to have children. Those children will have children, and there'll be problems, but we've made this decision." Drayton says, "What do you think is going to happen to your children? What does Joey think about this?" and Dr. Prentice says, "Well, Joey feels that every one of our children is going to be President of the United States and have a colorful administration. I think she's being a little optimistic. I'd say Secretary of State."

What's wonderful is the way William Rose has written this script; all his wonderful Irish wit dances about the serious points. And these *are* the points: the fact that the social structure is changing, the world is changing, that people are coming closer together. One hundred or two hundred years from now I don't think we're going to have any problems with racial differences. We're going to be all mixed up. We'll return to the original Adam, in a sense, whatever color he was. The differences will be eliminated, and people will not be judged by their superficial appearances, and I think this will be a wonderful, wonderful evolution.

Spencer Tracy

SELDOM during his career was Spencer Tracy a good subject for the interviewer. Like many truly great actors he never liked to talk about acting. It was something he "did." He had no theories about it. He also preferred not to talk about his private life, of friends or enemies, of the estrangement from his wife. Like his close friend and frequent costar, Katharine Hepburn, he compartmentalized his life to separate film star from man.

As I watched the film through the course of production I was anxious not to bug Tracy by insisting on a taping session. (The totality of his concentration and the short working schedule he followed, not a concern for his health, instigated this reticence. To me he looked in top condition.) But a day finally came when Spencer Tracy, led to some extent by Katharine, did sit down for a long taped interview. Since we worked between takes he jumped about a good deal from subject to subject, yet in this distillation much of the personality of Tracy emerges. Because it stands as his last interview, and the most extensive he every taped, it will be presented virtually intact.

SPENCER TRACY: Birth, Milwaukee, Wisconsin, Parochial grade schools, some time in Kansas City when my father was transferred, then back to Milwaukee and Marquette Academy. A stretch at Northwestern Military Academy, then Ripon College.

I suppose the whole business about appearing before the public began at Ripon, when I got on the debating team and we went on tour. The issue was the soldier's bonus and we had a great team. I hadn't had much of a chance to act in college—I was in one play, one real play, and thought it came off well—but the interest seemed to develop on its own. So on the way to debate up at Bowdoin College in Maine I went to the American Academy of Dramatic Arts and did an audition for Mr. Sargent, who was then head of the Academy. He was very nice—told me that if I wanted to come and attend I could do so, free, after I finished college. So after Ripon I went there for a year. Then I got a part in *R.U.R.* with the Theatre Guild, and things went along fairly well. I got jobs in stock and with Ethel Barrymore in New York, and in two or three other plays that had respectable runs.

My family didn't know what the hell to make of all this. My mother was for it, as mothers usually are, but my father wasn't at all pleased until I proved to be a brilliant actor. I hope you realize the word "brilliant" is a joke.

The big break came from George M. Cohan. I had played in stock with Selena Royle. She was in Cohan's company. A fellow with Cohan got fired, so Selena put in a plug for me, and another actor I knew said, "Oh,

I've seen Tracy, he's great." He hadn't seen me, but I've always been grateful to him for saying he had. Cohan sent for me and I got a part in *Yellow*. It ran for a year with Chester Morris. Then Cohan wrote *The Baby Cyclone* with a part for me.

I remember playing *The Baby Cyclone* in Boston the night Sacco and Vanzetti were electrocuted. The execution was to take place at midnight, and when I got out of the theater, at eleven o'clock, the Boston Common was filled with people protesting the execution. The undercurrent of violence was frightening. It's easy to see, after watching a thing like that, how mob hysteria can whip up riots or lynchings.

I remember, too, getting fired from a stock company in Providence. The manager said I had no sex appeal—this was after eight weeks with the outfit. He said, "The women don't want to come to see you at the matinee, but it wouldn't surprise me if someday you became a great motion-picture star. I said, "How the hell can I do that if I don't have any sex appeal?"

Later on I opened in a play in Providence. 1945. The play sold out all three nights, and I've always hoped the bastard tried to get in and couldn't get a ticket.

The Last Mile was my real smash hit, and while I was in it I made tests for all the studios—Universal, MGM, Fox, Warners. Nobody ever said a word—they never even called to tell me I was lousy. In those days they loaded you with makup for a screen test. I wasn't exactly pretty, anyway, so I probably ended up looking like a gargoyle. They most likely threw the film in the ashcan, but I didn't care very much because I never thought I'd be a movie actor; I had no ambition in that direction and was perfectly happy on the stage.

Then John Ford came to see the play, liked it, and took me out afterward. The next day he took me to see a fellow at Fox. Ford said, "I'd like to have him," and the Fox guy said, "Well, we made tests of him. They're not very good. He looks lousy in makeup." Ford said, "Makeup? He's not going to wear any makeup in my picture. He's the guy I want." When we got out of the office he told me how much money to ask for. I felt happily overpaid and came out here to Hollywood to do *Up the River* with Bogie and Clare Luce and Wiliam Collier. Bogie was the hero, and I was the villain.

I had a run-of-the-play contract with *The Last Mile,* but was off from June 1 through September 1, which was normal in those days, while I made the movie. We didn't finish fast enough and the studio tried to make a deal to keep me past September 1, but they wouldn't go for it. I ended up working day and night on the picture so that I could get back to New York to re-open in September. Finally the play closed, and I've been a movie actor, most of the time at least, ever since.

I still remember the opening night of *The Last Mile.* I was supposed to grab the guard to get the keys to unlock the cell, but that night the keys flew into the footlights. So I choked the guard a little more, grabbed his gun, and said, "Now, get those keys, you son-of-a-bitch!" the poor guy crawled down and got the keys and afterward, when I saw the marks on his neck, I realized I'd *really* choked him. He was damn near dead.

How have reviews affected you?

SPENCER TRACY: I don't think I've bothered too much about them. I can't remember any of the good reviews, and I don't remember all the bad ones. I've been roasted a few times, but not too often. I do recall that when *Dr. Jekyll and Mr. Hyde* opened at the Astor in New

York, one critic wrote, "Abbott and Costello opened at the Astor last night."

While I was making the picture, all dressed up for a scene with Ingrid Bergman, George Cukor brought Somerset Maugham on the set and explained that we were making *Jekyll and Hyde.* Maugham watched the scene and said, "Which part is he playing, now?"

Can you pick out those persons who've been most helpful, most influential, as far as your career is concerned?

SPENCER TRACY: Everyone has been important. Everybody I've worked with has been important to me. Everybody I've ever played with has meant something.

I read, not long ago, about an actor going on at great length about someone in the picture he was making who did things to upset him, upstage him, and so forth. I've never run into that sort of nonsense, not once. Nor do I think I've ever done it to anyone else. It never occurred to me. I should think this would be a very odd way to go about the business, to be worried all the time that somebody is trying to do you in, or to think about how to do someone else in. Good God, you have enough to concentrate on just to give a good performance.

They seem to talk a lot about this sort of behavior. But I have never come across it. The studios used to make up a lot of talk about feuds between people in the same movie, but they weren't true. Maybe this is because a movie is of fairly short duration in the making. Possibly, on the stage, if you go on year after year, you might develop terrible phobias against people just to stay awake. But in the picture industry—no. The effort seems to be to work together.

Have you noticed any difference in the industry since the big studios faded from power and the independents came up?

SPENCER TRACY: None at all. Maybe the reason is because I've been with Stanley Kramer for so long. The last six years I've been with him, and he runs things magnificently. He's actually a big-studio operation in himself, with creative priviliges the old established studio wouldn't have given him.

I miss MGM, but all the people I really knew there are gone. Scattered or dead. There's hardly anyone I know there, now. I'm the last of the tribe.

But even in the old days I didn't have the usual complaint about being forced to do pictures I didn't want to do. I never did a picture I didn't want to make. I've done some films that were bad, that I knew were bad, but if I'd refused to do them, I wouldn't have been suspended. In fact, I did turn down a few, and nothing drastic happened.

I've also been very fortunate with directors. No director has ever really bothered me or upset me. They tell me what to do, sometimes—not so much any more, because I've been around forever, and I should know the tricks—but they used to tell me what to do and I did it. I assumed they knew more about it than I did; I don't think you become a director overnight any more than you become an actor overnight. And the director has a hell of a lot more to do than the actor because he's got to keep the pieces together, not just one performance.

I made some tough pictures. Tough locations. *The Old Man and the Sea* wasn't an unmitigated pleasure. Three months in a little village outside Havana. *Northwest Passage* wasn't a picnic. The worst was *The Mountain*—the altitude gave us problems, and going up in the *têlêferique* was a nightmare. Once it stalled on us and swung against the side of the mountain while we looked down from thirteen thousand feet. Jeez! Later one of them dropped, hit by an airplane, and most of the people in the thing were killed.

Maybe I don't notice any real change in the industry because I've always concentrated totally and exclusively on the picture I've been doing at the moment. I'm not referring to any of this Method nonsense, either, but to the simple fact that you've got to know and feel a character in order to put him across believably. I read a great deal about the trials at Nuremberg before I did that picture. And when I did *Edison* I read all I could find about Edison. I went to Detroit to see Henry Ford, and he took me around the Edison museum, and I met Edison's widow and talked a great deal to his daughter. And I learned all I could about Father Flanagan before I did *Boy's Town.*

I researched the accent for *Captains Courageous* and thought I'd worked up a beaut until they brought a *real* Portuguese-American fisherman to me. We sat down in the director's office and I tried out my exotic new accent on him. I said, "Now, would you say 'leetle feesh'?" and he said, "No, I'd say 'little fish.' " So in the film, even though it got me an Academy Award, I probably had the most un-Portuguese accent in history. When I saw it at the Egyptian a guy patted me on the head and said, "All you needed was a derby hat." The makeup department gave me the works for that film—curly hair included. One day, just after I'd had my hair curled, I walked down the stairs at Metro and heard a scream. I looked up and Joan Crawford said, "My God, Harpo Marx!"

Could you draw a word portrait of Stanley Kramer? You've been closely associated with him for a longer time than you've been with any other producer or producer-director.

Spencer Tracy: Now, what the hell do you expect me to say? I'm in a picture with Stanley Kramer at the moment, and if I didn't like him, didn't admire him, I wouldn't be here.

I admire Stanley enormously. I think he does more, and tries harder, than anyone I know in this industry. He does things that are not always received wholeheartedly by the public. He's got the courage of his convictions at a time when few of us have courage and fewer of us have convictions. He's got guts. Certainly I wouldn't have done four pictures with Stanley if I I didn't think him the the greatest guy around.

It takes a special brand of courage, and of intelligence, and of taste, to do what Stanley has done. In fact, I don't think any other man could have dragged me back to the screen.

How thoroughly have you entered into the themes of pictures you've starred in, for instance, with Judgment at Nuremberg *or the racial theme in this picture?*

Spencer Tracy: I don't wave placards one way or the other. I read the script, and if I think it's a good script I'm anxious to do the picture. I happen to believe, as far as this picture is concerned, that integration is bound to take place, that this specific situation is bound to take place, but I don't look upon the picture as a "message." If there is one, fine. I certainly won't stand in its way. If there isn't, fine, too.

I think that any producer makes a mistake when he makes a picture in which the message comes first and the entertainment second. A movie is supposed to be an entertainment. If it says something important, in addition, all well and good. But if the message is there, but not the entertainment, people won't go to see it, so where the hell does the message go?

Is there a basic difference between the stars—as personalities—who were developed in the Metro heyday, and those coming up now?

SPENCER TRACY: Most of the old stars are gone. I'm about the only one left. It's completely different, now, because studios don't invest the time and money in personalities, the way they used to. Now they just bring them over from England.

But to talk about the differences between personalities and actors, and the nuances of personalities and actors, bores me stiff. I don't believe in the differences because I don't think they're important. And I agree with Laurence Olivier that it's a crashing bore to talk about acting. Who the hell knows anything about it? I don't. We've had some good authorities, including Edwin Booth, who haven't known. When Booth was asked what acting was, he said, "I haven't the faintest idea." And after thirty-five years I'd have to say "I haven't the faintest idea."

I remember when Bette Davis came to see me—we'd gotten Academy Awards about the same time, and she came on the set and said, "There's someone here who wants to interview me and they want to know what I think about acting, so I thought I'd come to you to get some ideas." I said, "Bette, you know better than that because I don't know what the hell I'm doing half the time." She said, "Neither do I, but I can't tell the guy that." I said, "Go ahead, tell him."

They talk about Method, overacting, underacting, style, all that. It's all a lot of crap. What any good actor does is crawl into the part he's playing and play it as completely as he can. He catches the character and is that character consistently.

But differences in actors—we're not as flamboyant, perhaps. They used to like us a little screwy, but now they like us colored gray.

As far as the press is concerned, how do you feel you've been treated?

SPENCER TRACY: Damned well, considering how little I've wanted to do with the press, and considering other things. They've been more than fair.

As far as fans—have you ever had the screaming, grabbing problem?

SPENCER TRACY: They've never grabbed me. I'm not pretty enough. The only demonstration I got involved in that was a little dangerous came when I took Elizabeth Taylor to the theater after we filmed *Father's Little Dividend*. That was in New York, and they damned near knocked the car over. But they weren't trying to get at me. Liz was the attraction. I got the "Can I have your autograph, who are you?" and the "Please sign fast so I can get the important stars" treatment. (Elizabeth was eighteen and nineteen in the two pictures we did together. She did her work and did it well; always knew what she was supposed to do. Great kid. And you think she's beautiful now? Sometimes, then, I'd watch her come down the stairs and I'd stare at her in absolute amazement. The beauty of that girl—incredible. And a wonderful girl. A wonderful woman.)

Once I was in New York at the same time Joan Crawford was there; we stayed at the same hotel. She called me and said, "You've been mean to your fans. There are several of them outside who just told me you've been very mean." (Joan used to let them follow her around when she was shopping.) And I said, "That's tough."

I'm not trying to downgrade fans, or say that I don't appreciate them. They keep you in pictures. But I think that a little distance should be involved. This "You've got two lapels, let me have one" business is for the birds.

What are your feelings regarding the Academy Awards, since you're one of the very few actors who has won two of them?

SPENCER TRACY: I believe in the nominations. I think the whole thing should end, however, with the five nominations, because I don't think you can pick a "best actor." It's enough of an honor to be one of the five nominees, but I don't see how you can compare performances accurately enough to single out one of the five as the best of the best.

I remember when Max Schell beat me out; we'd both been nominated for *Judgment at Nuremberg,* and he got up and thanked Kramer and everyone and then said, "But most of all, I want to thank that grand old man of the movies." I called him and said, "You son-of-a-bitch! I don't mind you winning the award, but calling me the grand old man, as if I'm some sort of ancient monument, is just too much!"

And when I got it for *Boys' Town* I got up and made a speech, something to the effect that they had really given the award to Father Flanagan, who was able to shine even through me, and I sat down to tremendous applause. Then someone came over and said, "I didn't see you in *Boys' Town* so I don't know whether you deserve the award, but you certainly deserve it for the performance you just gave."

But I really don't believe in picking the single "the best." How can you compare Michael Caine with Paul Scofield? Especially since Scofield spent half his life doing the part on the stage? Or Elizabeth Taylor with Lynn Redgrave? The pictures, the performances, are too different. The nomination is enough.

The other day, when you were talking about your earlier years in Hollywood, you mentioned Will Rogers.

SPENCER TRACY: We played polo together. We had lunch together nearly every day at Fox. He was a great man, a wonderful man, and when he was killed it sort of ended the polo, not only for me, but for a number of others. Nobody had the spirit after he was gone.

We used to go up to Will's house every Sunday and play; he had a polo field. I had to play under a phony name when we played at the Riviera because they had an audience, and if the studio heard I was playing they raised hell. But if "Max Slappenheimer" or "Amos McGurk" went up on the boards the studio couldn't squawk. But when Will went the polo went, too.

How do you react to seeing films you made a number of years ago?

SPENCER TRACY: I can't watch too many of them. I always see things I should have done differently, or better. It's downright spooky seeing yourself as you were twenty or thirty years ago when you were a completely different person, with the piss and vinegar you don't have now—and a lot of faults as a person you hope you've gotten over.

I don't think I've got an unusual fear of death, but I can't watch any film with Clark Gable or Bogie or any actor I knew well. (Maybe I do take death too seriously; I don't know.

I remember, when I was a kid, I shot a bird, and I cried so much over that goddam bird I could never hunt another thing.) Maybe I'm just too conscious of time passing, especially since I got so ill. But I can't watch the pictures I made with actors who are now dead. I'm too uncomfortable.

I spent a lot of time with Bogie before he died. My God, the way he stood up to it. Frank Sinatra would come over and we'd kid back and forth. Bogie would try so hard to be funny. Then one night I left and I said "Good night," as usual, but Bogie put his hand on mine and said, "Good-bye." He must have known something. I left his house completely shaken up, and sure enough, the next morning Bogie was dead.

But no—I can't watch the films I made with Clark, or Bogie, or the films they made. I'm probably too conscious of mortality. As I said, I'm the last of the tribe.

He was.

Spencer Tracy announced that *Guess Who's Coming to Dinner* would be his last film, that he was retiring, at the age of sixty-seven, from the screen. Katharine Hepburn disclaimed, "Oh, he says this after every picture."

This time Spencer meant what he said. A week later he died. *Guess Who's Coming to Dinner* will stand as the final performance given by the man other actors consistently regard as the greatest motion picture actor of all time.

Some reporters, after his death, speculated that overwork on the film had killed him. While it is true that his part was a demanding one, filled with long speeches and climaxed by a challenging six-and-one-half-page "soliloquy" at the end (a speech few actors could have brought off), it is also true that Tracy's health, for the past five years, had veered from a close approach to death to the reassuring heartiness he felt while filming this production.

During the movie everyone who knew Tracy or who had worked with him (some publicity and crewmen went back twenty years or more to share his heyday at Metro) claimed he looked better than he had in decades. Moreover, Stanley Kramer had scheduled Tracy's working hours to let him come in at ten in the morning and leave shortly after lunch. Zero hour was four o'clock, and Tracy seldom worked that late. He watched his diet, didn't drink or smoke, and freely admitted how he looked forward to the single bottle of Danish beer he allowed himself before dinner. He rested between takes, sometimes joking quietly with costars or members of the crew.

The shock of Spencer Tracy's death is not lessened by the fact that he lived at a time and acted in the medium that guarantees a measure of immortality. Garrick and Booth, Modjeska and Bernhardt, said their lines upon the wind, and none of their words were recorded, none of their poses made fluid by film. Even today when we see the earliest of Tracy's films we can appreciate his work and are thankful that it can be preserved for posterity.

Filmed immortality will also serve Tracy well because he came of age at a time when strutting and posturing went out of style. The naturalness of his work, the immersion in character, stands little chance of being outdated. (It has taken theater an eternity, after all, to recognize the depth of communication that comes through believability; it is doubtful if this particular pendulum will swing back to wide-eyed melodrama or exotic romanticizing.)

It is appropriate that *Guess Who's Coming to Dinner* stands as Spencer Tracy's last picture. His forte was contemporary comedy-drama, and this film is a choice example of that genre. He loved a good script, and Bill Rose wrote a gem. He admired independence and courage, and Stanley Kramer supplied these qualities. He loved and respected great actors, and he had both Hepburn and Poitier to share honors with him throughout a satisfying production schedule.

He was, indeed, the last of his tribe, the last of the superstars who made the screen an art form with a commercial guarantee. And thanks to film neither Manuel nor Father Flanagan, nor Thomas Edison nor Matt Drayton will disappear, and the man who was Tracy will become the legend that *is* Tracy, and it will be gratifying.